# GOD AND MEN

# GOD & MEN

By
### HERBERT H. FARMER

## ABINGDON-COKESBURY PRESS
*New York* ● *Nashville*

# GOD AND MEN

SET UP, ELECTROTYPED, PRINTED, AND BOUND
BY THE PARTHENON PRESS AT NASHVILLE
TENNESSEE, UNITED STATES OF AMERICA

# PREFACE

THE SUBSTANCE of these chapters was delivered—under the title "The Christian Message and the World of Persons"—as the Lyman Beecher Lectures at the Divinity School of Yale University in April, 1946. I desire to acknowledge once again the honor which the authorities of the Divinity School showed me in inviting me to give the lectures, and to thank them for their warm kindness to me during my stay among them.

In preparing the material for publication I have made a number of minor alterations and additions, some of them in the light of questions asked. But the purpose of the lectures, as well as the limitation on their length, must still explain some—though I fear not nearly all—of the deficiencies and omissions of the book.

Although the Lyman Beecher lectureship was originally founded to deal with the subject of "Preaching," it is now expressly permitted to take up any theme appropriate to the work of the Christian minister. Obviously a purely theological topic falls under that description; nevertheless, among many possible theological topics the choice should be guided, I think, by the task of preaching and the needs of preachers at this present time. Such an approach not only keeps reasonably close to the intention, the name, and the tradition of the lectureship, but also coincides with my own impulse and desire. I find it increasingly hard to be interested in a theological discussion the bearing of which on the actual business of being a Chris-

5

tian in this tragic modern world—and the bearing of which, therefore, on the preacher's task of calling, and helping, men and women to be Christians in that world— I am not able to discern. Thus the theme of this book was chosen because it seemed to me to bear directly and vitally on the task of presenting the Christian message to our day and generation.

While these pages are meant to be of some help, if possible, to working ministers in their difficult and responsible task of making the Christian message living and credible to ordinary men and women today, they may also be of help to any of such ordinary men and women who may chance to read them. By "ordinary" in this connection I mean unversed in technical theology and theological terms, and unaware, for the most part, of the deeper theological and philosophical problems which underlie the great verities of our faith; I have tried to bear such people in mind all through.

Since my purpose has been to bring together some of the main elements in Christian teaching, in order to illustrate what I have called its radical personalism, there has been at a few points a slight repetition of things I have said elsewhere in a different context and for a different purpose. I hope this may be pardoned.

It will be observed that I have continually used some such phrase as "the Christian message affirms," or "Christianity teaches," and this may perhaps give an impression of overconfident dogmatism, especially on some points. Yet always to add a qualifying phrase such as "according to my understanding of it" would be very irksome to the

reader. I can only express the hope that all that I have said
—while it must necessarily bear the stamp, and exhibit
the deficiencies, of my own thought—is sufficiently in
harmony with the substance of the faith, as it has been
wrought out down the centuries of Christian thought and
experience in the Church, to make the phrases referred
to not altogether without justification.

I am especially indebted to the Rev. A. Whigham
Price for reading the manuscript and helping to reduce
considerably my many infelicities of style and presentation. I am also grateful to Miss O. Macdonald for typing
the lectures.

HERBERT H. FARMER

# CONTENTS

tent, omniscient, omnipresent, (iv) eternal, (v) infinite perfection.

# Chapter I

# THE WAY OF KNOWLEDGE

THE CONTEMPORARY situation and the contemporary mind being what they are, it is most important that the great verities of the Christian revelation be so presented and taught that three conditions at least are fulfilled.

First, they should be so presented that the *massive unity and consistency* of the Christian view, taken in its whole range and depth, are made clear and intelligible. The scrappy, disconnected, and only half-understood bits of Christian doctrine which so many people both inside and outside the churches take to be what they vaguely call "Christianity" are of little more use in the turmoil and perplexity of this time than would be a few scattered heaps of stones as a breakwater on a stormy coast.

Second, they should be so presented that the *distinctiveness* of the Christian view is made unmistakably plain. By the word "distinctiveness" I mean to imply that what Christianity teaches about God and man—taken, I repeat, in its whole range and depth—sets it apart from all other interpretations of human life which, in one form or another, today compete for the acceptance and allegiance of men. There is no substitute, or near substitute, for it; nor, without ceasing to be itself, can it be merged in anything else in a sort of amalgam. I mean to imply also that there is in the Christian message

11

that which inevitably puts it in sharp opposition to, and protest against, much that, consciously or unconsciously, rules men's minds in our time. If Christian people are not soundly and comprehensively instructed in the truth, they will be unaware of this "apartness" and opposition, and their minds will be correspondingly defenseless against the infiltrations of a contemporary culture which is profoundly non-Christian, and even anti-Christian, but which they fail to recognize as such.

This happens more frequently than we realize. We are all the children of our time, and the danger is always present that we shall be this so unconsciously and uncritically that, without being aware of it, we shall cease to be what the New Testament calls "the children of light, and the children of the day." No doubt it is right that we should be the children of our time—for indeed we cannot very well be anything else. Moreover we are under obligation to seek to present the truth in a way which modern folk can grasp and which makes evident its relevance to the important concerns of their life. We are also under obligation to keep abreast, so far as possible, of relevant modern knowledge, so that we may not miss anything that God may give us through it for the purging and enrichment of our apprehension of the faith. Being modern, and speaking to modern minds, we must make a *modern* presentation of the Christian message. But we must be very alert to see that it is the *Christian* message we present, and that none of its essential distinctiveness is sacrificed to the desire to be "up to date."

12

Third, it is vitally important to present the great verities of our faith in such wise that *their radical and consistent personalism* is convincingly set forth. The full import of the italicized phrase will become clearer, it is hoped, in what follows. At this point I will only state my conviction that in this matter of its intense personalism we are confronted with a central issue, perhaps *the* central issue, in the relations of Christian truth to the contemporary mind. It is this which more than anything else runs counter to that culture[1] which in the West has largely displaced the Christian culture of previous centuries, and which makes Christian belief difficult, even when the need is felt for some kind of religious faith in face of the grim events of these times. I have tried to set forth elsewhere some of the causes of this difficulty in believing the personalist teaching of Christianity—causes rooted in the whole setup of our contemporary life and by no means exclusively, or even mainly, of a reflective or intellectual kind.[2] Nevertheless—and this is another reason why this is a central issue—in spite of the truth of what has just been said, I believe that it is precisely by showing more effectively than we have perhaps hitherto done the profound implication of the Christian message in the world of persons and personal relationships that we are most likely to overcome this difficulty in belief, and make the message come alive in people's minds.

[1] I use the word "culture" in a broad sense to indicate the more or less settled ways of thought and feeling which govern the life of a community and shape its members without their being aware of it.

[2] In an article contributed to the volume *Has The Church Failed?* (1947) , ed. by Sir. J. Marchant. Others have dealt more fully with the matter, notably Berdyaev, in *Slavery and Freedom* (1943) .

The two statements just made are not contrary to one another. To maintain that the point of greatest challenge and difficulty is also the point of greatest hope is perhaps merely another way of maintaining, as we must, that the truth has its permanent allies in the human soul and the human situation, however ineffective these allies may temporarily appear to be. Or again it is perhaps another way of saying that, whatever place there may be for the argumentative rebuttal of contrary views—and I would by no means deny that there is such a place—nevertheless in all that concerns the ultimate truths and values of our life the only way in the end to rout the forces of error is to lead in, and effectively deploy, the forces of truth. In short, the strongest apologetic, so far as preaching and teaching are concerned, is always a sound dogmatic. Those, therefore, who seek to commend Christianity to our contemporaries by toning down, or explaining away, or translating into other terms, its uncompromisingly personalist view of God and man fall into a double error. On the one hand they really destroy the essence of the message they desire to commend, and on the other hand they defeat the very purpose they are seeking to achieve. If modern folk find it hard to respond to the personalism of Christianity, there is not the least evidence—rather the contrary—that they will find it any easier to respond to an impersonalized version, or perversion, of it.

It is with these thoughts in mind that I have chosen my theme. My endeavor will be to set forth some of the elements of the Christian teaching concerning God and man so that the three conditions just laid down are in a measure fulfilled—that is to say, so that the radical personalism of the Christian message, its distinctiveness over against contemporary modes of thought, its unity and consistency, are made plain. I hope that in so doing I may be of some help to those whose task is to preach and teach the message.

This being the aim, the method has been chosen in harmony with it. In my exposition I shall have in mind all the time—and in a measure be speaking directly to— not so much convinced and instructed Christian believers, still less expert theologians, but, as it were, an imaginary audience of modern men and women. I shall especially have in mind young men and women who are serious-minded enough to listen to what Christianity has to say, but in whom there are at work those influences of our time which make Christian belief, to say the least, not easy for them. Yet, even so, that will be in some measure to address those who would wish to be counted Christian believers; for, as I have said, we are all children of our time, and subject more than we know to its climate.

In accordance with this general aim and method I shall try to avoid technical theological language, and shall make no attempt to deal with the theological problems involved in a complete and thoroughgoing way. It is rather the general shape of the wood, and what this implies as to the right way to approach and explore it, that I want to make clear; to do this we must not give too much time to examining individual trees—if the familiar metaphor may be allowed in spite of the ineptitude of comparing the Christian revelation to anything so dim and entangling as a wood.

I have just spoken of the right way to approach and explore the Christian teaching. This is a matter of such consequence in relation to the task of presenting the truth to men and women today that I propose to dwell on it throughout this chapter. The content of the Christian message being what it is, we are entitled to ask that it be approached from the beginning in a certain attitude of mind. So long as this attitude is withheld—as it is not infrequently withheld—little progress can be made.

## I

First, if the truth of the Christian message is to come home to a man, he must bring to it the most serious mind he can command.

He must bring a mind which is aware, and aware all the time, of how much is at stake in the matter; a mind which is striving to keep itself open and responsive to the great things of life—one which has, in the phrase which Morley used of Burke, "a grave diligence for high things"; a mind which realizes that if it is a serious matter to believe in the God set forth in the Christian message, as it most certainly is to anyone who really believes in him, it is an equally serious matter *not* to believe in him—that in short, the decision between belief and unbelief is a very grave decision, particularly in such a time as this.

The greatest respect is due to any man who, after sincere and prolonged consideration of what Christianity has to say—a consideration continually renewed as his experience grows and deepens—still finds that he cannot accept it. But none is due to the man who brings to the whole matter a casual, flippant, feet-on-the-mantlepiece attitude; or raises the obvious difficulties but never stays to consider whether there are not less obvious answers to them —less obvious because they go deeper, because they have to do with the deepest of all realities, which is God; or will not take the trouble to acquaint himself with what the Christian view in its wholeness really is, but is content to judge it on the basis of some sketchy and garbled account of it—which, as likely as not, he picked up in a Sunday-school class ten or twenty years ago, and has in any case more than half forgotten since then. The latter attitude is not uncommon, even in people who ought to know better. It is as though a man should set up as a judge of dramatic art on the basis of having once seen in his youth a Punch and Judy show.

The utterly unscientific attitude sometimes displayed by professedly scientific men in this regard is particularly exasperating; their statements about Christian belief show clearly that they do not know what they are talking about, have never taken the trouble, and do not intend to take the trouble, to find out what they are talking about—an attitude of mind which they would scorn if they met it in their own chosen scientific field. There is in this not only a failure in scientific conscience and responsibility, but also a failure in what may be called cultural sensitivity—though I am not wishing in the least to suggest that such a failure is peculiar to, or usually characteristic of, scientific men; it is not.

17

Throughout the history of Western thought, right down to the present hour, there has been an uninterrupted succession of superlatively great minds in philosophy, in science, and in other spheres who, with inevitable individual differences, *have* believed in God in the Christian sense of that term. One need only mention such names as Aquinas, Descartes, Leibniz, Kant, Newton, Lotze, Faraday, Maxwell, Eddington, out of many more. To dismiss without serious and informed consideration that which held the allegiance of such minds is, after all, the merest philistinism.

Moreover, whatever we may be led to believe or not to believe about God, the word "God" most certainly comes to us from out of the past charged with some of the most poignant feelings and experiences of those who have gone before us; it comes charged with the hopes and fears, the heroisms and sacrifices, of countless men and women, known and unknown. No doubt it comes charged with other things as well, for evil and horrible things have been done in the name of God; but nothing can alter the fact that the word is soaked, if I may so put it, in the tears of suffering humanity and in the blood of martyrs and saints. To meet it, therefore, with anything less than our most serious and painstaking mind is to fail in sensitivity; it is to lack a "grave diligence for high things."

## II

Second, if the truth of the Christian message is to come home to a man, he must bring to it a certain practical alertness and expectancy.

18

This necessity arises from the fact that in the systematic exposition of Christian truth we are bound to use abstract terms and make highly generalized statements; we are bound also to be in a measure argumentative; and we are certainly under obligation to be as strictly logical as we can. The intellectual side of us is chiefly called into action. But this means that the very reality which is the object of our thought—namely, the nature and purpose of God as these are apprehended in Christian faith—is in some measure obscured and falsified.

For if the Christian view is true, then, whatever else God is, he is a personal reality who stands in a quite peculiar, profound, and inescapable relationship to every man as an individual—that is, whole—person. He makes, as we shall see later, a certain all-inclusive and absolute claim upon our whole being—all the time and in all circumstances whatsoever—and with that claim, and our response to it, our whole destiny is bound up. It is precisely this that constitutes him the living, personal God; and only in so far as a man apprehends in some measure this direct and unique relationship to himself can he be said to be apprehending, in any way that is of the least consequence to himself or to anybody else, the reality of God. The defect of the abstract, theoretical, generalized approach of the lecture room is that it inevitably tends to sidetrack or obscure this relationship.[3] God becomes an object to be talked about in general terms at an arranged hour instead of a personal being who continually ad-

---

[3] This is not so true of the sermon, set as it is in a context of worship, prayer and fellowship, though it is true in some degree of it also.

dresses us in the precise and particular terms of our individual lives. And this, I repeat, in so far as it takes place, seriously obscures and falsifies the absolutely distinctive reality which we designate by the term "God." It is as though one put on glasses in order to examine the properties of steam; the glasses—useful as they are in countless other ways—in this particular instance mist up, clouding and distorting the reality they are meant to reveal.

The only remedy is for a man always to bring with him to the consideration of the Christian message what I have called a practical alertness and expectancy. He must, as it were, continually wipe his glasses by asking himself this question: What has all this, if it is true, to do with me as a person in some measure in charge of his own destiny—which destiny is certainly wrought, not in listening to, and arguing about, lectures and sermons, but in the practical choices of everyday existence where decisions have to be made and the consequences of decisions endured?

We might express the point thus: No one should expect to be able first to decide whether what is said about God is true, and thereafter to decide its practical relevance to himself; rather it is only by seeing in some degree its relevance to himself that he can ever be in a position rightly to decide the question of its truth.

## III

Third, if the truth of the Christian message is to come home to a man, he must bring to it a certain sincerity and singleness of mind.

It is important in this connection to realize that in the last resort there is only one reason for believing anything to be true, and that is that we cannot *help* believing it to be true. At some point or other truth must shine in its own light, must lay hold of the mind with direct, compelling power, so that a man feels that he has no option but to say, "Yes, that is true, and I cannot honestly deny that it is true." If this needs further elucidation, we have only to consider that we should otherwise be in a state of mind in which, in point of fact, nobody outside a lunatic asylum ever is—a state of mind in which everything is questioned and nothing whatever is ever asserted or denied; a state of mind in which no argument would ever come to any end, for nothing could be established— indeed, no serious argument could ever begin, for there would be no reason for starting with one set of premises rather than another. There is an approach to such a state of mind in certain mental diseases—the Germans call it *Grübelsucht,* the French *folie de doute*—in which the patient is incapable of believing anything. In its extremer developments there is total disintegration of the mind.

This ultimate, intrinsic compellingness of truth, however, does not mean that anything that lays hold of the mind with convincing power is in fact always and necessarily true, so that there is no need to examine it or think any more about it; for experience shows that it is possible for false beliefs thus to take possession of men's minds. No doubt it is overwhelmingly obvious to the lunatic that he is Julius Cæsar, but it is nevertheless not true. This possibility of false certainties does not, however, affect the main point, which is that, in the end, both for the sane and for the not so sane, both for those who are thinking truly and for those who happen in fact to be thinking falsely, the appeal must be to our own immediate sense of truth, and by its verdict we must abide and be prepared to act.

Nor, on the other hand, does it mean that we are *not* entitled to believe anything that does not immediately shine in its own light, anything that cannot be seen to be true by direct inspection. That manifestly would be absurd. For example, I am quite convinced that the proposition that the three angles of any triangle together make up two right angles is true. But I certainly do not discern this by direct inspection; the proposition, taken in isolation, does not immediately authenticate itself to me, when I understand its terms, by its own self-evidencing power. It is not difficult to see, however, that, *taken in its appropriate setting and context*—the context of Euclid's proof—it does, along with its context, shine in its own light. I begin the proof with intuitions and axioms which I cannot question; I move by rational steps, each of which I cannot question, to the conclusion that the three angles together equal two right angles; and that conclusion, grasped along with the premises and the argumentative steps, now shares in their unquestionability. All through the proof I rely on the self-evidencing power of truth; and if anyone were mentally big enough to take in the theorem—axioms, inferences, and conclusion—at a single glance, the whole thing would be immediately intuited as self-evident.

The appeal then must always be *to* a man's direct sense of truth, and therefore *for* a certain sincerity and singleness of mind in relation to it. If anyone is disposed, for one reason or another, to be really obstinately skeptical about it all, to develop a touch of *Grübelsucht,* to go on arguing and arguing, casting around for ever-new difficulties and questions with which at once to dim the light of assent and conviction so soon as it begins to shine and take possession of the mind, there is little point in going on. It is not suggested, of course, that questions should not be asked or difficulties raised. I have already said that things which *appear* to be true may in fact prove to be false. But there is a difference between facing questions which force themselves on us with something of the compulsion of reality and truth behind them, and thinking up questions in order, if possible, to escape the compulsion of reality and truth. It is the difference between sincere and insincere thought; and if anybody says he does not know the difference, I do not know any way to make clear what it is. Even that difference must shine in its own light.

## IV

Fourth, if the truth of the Christian message is to come home to a man, it must always be set in an adequate context. The context must be wide and deep. This seems to follow from the notion of God itself, as this is understood by Christianity. For if by "God" we mean that final reality of righteousness and love from which all things, including ourselves, depend for their existence, their nature, their coherence, their unfolding history, and final outcome, then the whole meaning of our existence is at stake in him, and nothing less than the whole breadth of our experience could be the appropriate and sufficient context for thinking about him.

I do not mean by this that only people of wide experience and knowledge are entitled to believe in God—which would be manifestly absurd. But I do mean that, even if a man has a relatively narrow experience, the proper context for him in which to try to set the Christian view of God—if he is prepared to think about it at all—must always be the whole extent of that experience such as it is; and he must always be trying to widen his experience. Nor do I mean that a vivid and compelling sense of God may not be given to a man through a relatively restricted section or area of his life and experience; that also is plainly not the case. It is a commonplace of religious experience that some things in life do speak much more plainly to us of God than others; there are moments of particularly vivid insight and conviction. But I do say that such insight and conviction are not securely possessed until they are set in a much wider context of experience, shedding light upon that context and themselves reciprocally receiving light from it. Indeed, I would say that we are under obligation to set them in this wider context. For, as we have seen, a belief is not necessarily true because it lays hold of the mind with a certain intrinsic compelling power—even though, as we have also seen, we have in the end no other criterion of truth than the truth's own power to convince.

It is important to insist that in this matter of belief in God we really must study large maps and take deep soundings, because people, even intelligent people, are so ready to dispose of the matter on much too narrow a basis. It will be well to give some examples.

Thus, the demand is sometimes made—in effect, if not in so many terms—that the existence of God should be cogently demonstrated by an argument of the same conclusive type as that by which, to use the same illustration again, the three angles of a triangle can be shown to be together equal to two right angles. Prove the existence of God, it is said; and by "prove" is meant: Start with absolutely indubitable facts, proceed through absolutely unquestionable inferences to an absolutely irresistible conclusion. No such proof being forthcoming, the decision then is, apparently, that God is not real, or, at least, that there is no adequate reason for believing him to be real.

Yet surely if God is indeed the sort of reality that Christianity believes him to be—namely, the creative, righteous, trustworthy purpose who rules all things to good ends, and claims us for his service in complete obedience and trust—if the whole meaning of our mixed and troubled existence as persons who have wills to decide, and consciences to judge between good and evil, and feelings to be uplifted by great enterprises and reverences, as well as harassed and tormented at times by great sufferings, is in him; then a neat little packet of abstract logic surely could not be sufficient to authenticate his reality to us. How could you prove by a syllogism, or by a whole series of syllogisms, to a man suffering from cancer

that all things work together for good—that all things
past, all things present (including the cancer), all things
to come, are grasped by an infinite and austere purpose of
love which he can trust, and through faith in which he
can win the victory? It seems evident it cannot be done.
The conclusion to be reached is too big, too deep, too
all-inclusive, too much bound up with both the heights
and the depths of our nature and experience, to be established—or rejected—on such a narrow foundation of
abstract ratiocination.

Take another example. One not infrequently meets
people who are apparently quite prepared to justify their
dismissal of the Christian view of God on the grounds
that some, or even many, of the Christian believers whom
they have met are not markedly superior in character and
conduct to others who make no such profession at all, and
are sometimes, indeed, positively inferior to them. Now I
certainly would not wish to exclude consideration of the
difference which belief in God makes to human life and
character from that total context of thought and experience in relation to which the truth of such belief can alone
be properly assessed. The argument is not beside the point.
But it is surely obvious that such considerations by themselves, resting as they must on the chances and super-
ficialities of casual personal encounter and acquaintance,
are a most inadequate ground on which to dispose of so
vast and deep a question. When such considerations are
introduced, let them take a broader sweep and be carried
to a deeper level than that.

Let there be an examination, for example, of the

evidence which history, as it is wrought out over many generations, offers as to the relation of the Christian interpretation of God and man to the ethical level of human life. Let us take note of the collapse and disintegration of European civilization which has gradually followed upon the widespread decay of Christian belief, and has reached a ghastly climax in this our day. Let us ponder, so far as we are able, the thought of men like Christopher Dawson, Reinhold Niebuhr, Jacques Maritain, Nikolai Berdyaev. The matters set forth by such writers are, in their breadth and depth, to say the least, a good deal more commensurate with the Christian idea of God and the momentous decision which confronts modern men in respect of belief in him, than is the fact that Mr. Smith, who makes some sort of profession of Christianity, already beats his wife, whereas Mr. Brown, who makes no such profession, has not so far begun to do so. Here also it is most necessary to study large maps and take deep soundings.[4]

Another example: It has to do with the evil in the world. Nobody—least of all today—would wish to minimize the challenge which the evil of life offers to belief in the good purpose of God. The Christian faith certainly insists that we should face it, and has some deep things to say about it. But the point is that the proper setting for thought about God ought to include a good deal more than the manifest and obtrusive evils of our life. Not to speak of other things, it ought to include the good, and

[4] I have discussed elsewhere the relation of Christian belief in God to the fundamental problems of individual life. See *Towards Belief in God* (1942), Chaps. V and VI.

above all the overcoming of evil through faith in God. And the further point is that too often people do not see this. They are content to dispose of the question of belief in God on the basis of a consideration of evil, or even of one particularly disturbing and startling example of it, in abstraction from all else. They make no attempt either to widen the context to include the great things of life or to deepen their insight in relation to the evil itself. The statement of a certain well-known writer, "I do not believe in God because there is such a thing as a cholera microbe," may no doubt be taken to reveal a heart sensitive to human suffering; but considered as an argument sufficient in itself to dispose of belief in the God of whom the Christian faith speaks, it must be characterized as extremely shallow and superficial.

This last point leads to a further thought. Among the great things of life which ought always to be included in the context of a man's thought about God are the infinite depth and mystery of the universe in which he finds himself alive. In a world which had not this fourth dimension of mystery, of the unfathomed and uncomprehended, the Christian religion, perhaps religion in any form, could not live at all. In Rudolf Otto's words, "It could not sail on its shallow waters, or breathe its thin air." The very notion of God includes mystery as part of its essential meaning—*deus cognitus, deus nullus:* known God, no God—and a man is hardly in a fit state to think about God if he does not already acknowledge and abase himself before the immense mystery of the world of which he is a part, and on which he utterly depends. To achieve, and to retain, this sense of the profundity and mystery of existence appears to require an effort on the part of some modern folk, born and bred as they are amid the artificialities of city life and too often conditioned by a narrowly scientific and technical education to think that only the rationally transparent and comprehensible is worthy of credence or likely to contribute to human well-being. Nevertheless, it is an effort we must ask, and expect, them to make.

The point I am making is, however, not understood if it is taken to mean simply that a man should acknowledge —because he must, and perhaps with regret—that there is much we do not know and cannot know. Such an agnosticism, which need be little more than a recognition of obvious fact, is quite compatible with an irreligious, rationalistic humanism, and is not necessarily a preparation for the Christian message. It can, indeed, easily pass over into a dogmatic agnosticism which refuses to think about God at all because by definition he so greatly transcends human thought. Rather what I am pleading for is an attitude of mind which is prepared to rejoice in the mysterious depths of reality, which indeed counts such mystery among "the great things of life" and would not have it otherwise, any more than one would want Rembrandt's pictures without their dense shadows. In short, I would have a man bring to the consideration of Christian truth whatsoever of reverence and humility he can already find within his soul.

This must not be misinterpreted. I do not mean that we are not to seek to probe the mysteries of our life and world. Only by seeking to probe them can we realize their depth. I am not arguing for any sort of stark irrationalism, or for an unteachable obscurantism. The point is simply that the presence of the unillumined and unexplained in our experience ought never to be taken as *by itself* sufficient to invalidate, to make unreasonable and insincere, belief in God. For the question remains whether the thought of God, as mediated through the Christian revelation, does not, when taken in the total setting of a man's life, still lay hold of his being with constraining force; and does so, not merely in spite of the unillumined mysteries, but also in some measure because they are there.

## V

Finally, if the truth of the Christian message is to come home to a man, he must bring to it somthing of the spirit of adventure.

I not infrequently observe—especially in "laboratory-trained" minds—what seem to me to be wholly mistaken ideas concerning what is reasonable or unreasonable in relation to belief in God. There is what appears to be a false and finicky intellectual conscience, amounting at times to a kind of intellectual conceit. Let me explain: There is a sense in which a man cannot take too seriously his responsibility for his beliefs, and this high enterprise of seeking truth and ridding himself of untruth; to be able to set that aim before the mind is indeed what marks man out as a creature having reason—by "reason" I suppose we mean, in part at least, the power deliberately to set truth before the mind as an end to be sought. But, on the other hand, it is possible in another sense to take this responsibility too seriously, or rather to take it seriously in the wrong way, so that we defeat the purpose in view, which is the acquisition of truth.

An example from another sphere will help to make this clear. It is undoubtedly a duty to take care of our health —to take exercise, to eat proper food, to avoid obvious sources of infection, and so on. Now I once knew a lady who took this obligation so seriously that she became an intolerable burden to herself and to everybody else, and in the end completely defeated her own intention. She developed a false and finicky hygienic conscience—a sort of hygienic conceit: she would never use a telephone without wiping the mouthpiece with disinfectant; she took her own cup with her wherever she went; she made a point of washing out her own, and her children's, insides with drugs and purgatives of singular and often quite unpredictable potency. She lived in perpetual fear of picking up germs. The result was, as might have been expected, she was continually picking them up.

In a similar way it is possible to develop a false and finicky intellectual conscience and conceit which similarly defeat the true end of reason and intelligence. It is possible to take our obligation in all things to find truth and avoid error in such a way that we do in fact find error and avoid truth. I will give two illustrations of what I mean.

The first takes the form of asserting, in effect, that we are not entitled, as rational beings responsible for what we believe, to acquiesce in any proposition against which it is possible to raise demurrers and questions, or even to

31

accept any proposition the opposite of which can be entertained by the mind as a theoretical possibility. If this were a sound principle, then, for me at least, belief in God would have to go. For that it is possible to raise serious demurrers to belief in God, not all of which can be answered in a completely satisfactory way, I cannot deny; nor can I deny that the unreality of God is, in the present state of our knowledge, a theoretical possibility— that is to say, it is possible to assert it without logical self-contradiction. But is such a principle sound? I maintain it is not sound. On the contrary, from the point of view of our responsibility as reasonable beings to desire and seek truth, it is a thoroughly unreasonable principle. Its unreasonableness is shown by the fact that it really unfits us for the very enterprise in whose interest it is invoked. It leads to the missing of truth, rather than the discovery of it.

Incidentally, it is a principle on the basis of which none of us could live our lives for a single day, or even hour. We have continually to accept as "true," propositions which theoretically could be false and may in fact prove so—propositions the negation of which it is possible to assert without logical self-contradiction. It is theoretically conceivable that the sun will not rise tomorrow; at any rate the proposition that it will not do so is not an intrinsically ridiculous or self-contradictory one. But if I refused to commit myself to the truth that it will rise, because of the abstract theoretical possibility that it will not, I should obviously be a very foolish and unreasonable person indeed.

What is wrong with this attitude is that it conceals a

fear, at once cowardly and intellectually conceited, of falling into error, precisely as the lady I have just referred to had a fear of collecting germs. And just as she missed the positive blessings of health by the negative and self-protective attitude of seeking to avoid disease, so this attitude may very well miss certain grand and emancipating truths—truths which do in fact have a certain self-authenticating power to us in our less sophisticated and self-conscious intellectualist moods, and which would increasingly authenticate themselves if, taking the risks of error, we would adventurously commit ourselves to them.

William James put the point effectively many years ago in an essay which it is still a tonic to read.[5] I venture to condense and paraphrase his remarks. He maintains that either we may regard the pursuit of truth as paramount, and the avoidance of error secondary; or we may, on the other hand, treat the avoidance of error as more imperative, and let truth take its chance. The former attitude says in effect: The risk of being in error is a very small matter when compared with the blessing of real knowledge; I am ready to be duped many times rather than postpone forever the chance of knowing truth. The latter attitude says in effect: Believe nothing that anybody can ever raise a doubt about or that your own mind can question; keep your mind in suspense forever; say, I don't know, I am agnostic, rather than incur the awful risk of believing error. But this is really fantastic; it is like a general's informing his soldiers that it is better to keep out of the battle forever rather than run the risk of a

[5] *The Will to Believe* (1899), Essay I.

single wound. Not so are victories won over our enemies.

Worse things can happen to a man than to believe an untruth. For one thing, an untruth may have a deeper truth wrapped up in it; it may be a distorted and partial statement of that deeper truth, so that the only way to come at the deeper truth is to try to live by the error. Surely our errors are not necessarily such enormously solemn things. In a world where we are certain to incur them in spite of all our caution, a certain adventurousness is healthier and more reasonable than this excessive nervousness. The fact is, agnosticism, which often parades itself as intellectual modesty, can easily veil an intellectual laziness and cowardice and self-conceit. As Oman has said: "So far is reality from feeling obliged to meet all our objections that it only dimly unveils itself to our most sympathetic and far-reaching [adventurous] insight. This may be highly unphilosophical on the part of our environment, yet the fact remains, and even philosophy can only accept it." [6]

The other example is perhaps more characteristic of this present time. Psychologists have so dinned into us the ever-present danger of wishful thinking, of believing that a thing is true because we want very much that it should be true, of "escapism" as it is called—and indeed the danger is obvious enough without the psychologists—that it has induced in many minds an error of an opposite but equally disabling kind: the error of refusing to believe anything that meets and satisfies human desires and needs —even though they may be needs and desires, not of a

[6] *The Natural and the Supernatural* (1931), p. 52.

merely egotistic or transient kind, but such as are bound up with the total significance of our life and our destiny as persons. Many moderns appear to have made the phrase "too good to be true" into something approaching a regulative principle of knowledge and belief. Of two propositions, they say in effect, choose always to believe the more cheerless and depressing.

Now of course it is advisable to be on our guard against wishful thinking; our wishes and desires may, and not infrequently do, fog reality. But then equally much our wishes and desires, if they are of the right sort, may be an indispensable factor in knowing realities of a certain order. Why not? They are part of the real world, and there is certainly truth of feeling as well as truth of exact logical statement and proof. Of course the fact that you would like a proposition to be true is not a good reason for believing it, apart from any further evidence; but then, equally, the fact that you would like it to be true is not by itself a very good reason for *dis*believing it. An exaggerated fear of being the dupe of your own desires may itself be a sort of inverted wishful thinking. Fear after all is an emotion and usually a very egotistic one, and if emotion can fog reality in the one case, it can in the other; "If hopes were dupes, fears may be liars." Or as James puts it in the essay already referred to: "Dupery for dupery, what proof is there that dupery through hope is so much worse than dupery through fear?"

The attitude reveals, once again, an unreasonable fear of falling into error, and it leads to the missing of great and glorious tracts of truth. It is, or at least can be, a form of intellectual pride and conceit: "I at least among all these silly believers will not be duped!" And it very easily runs out into a supine and lazy agnosticism, which says: "I don't know, I can't know, and I don't propose to take any risks in trying to find out."

There is, however, this further which must be said. The notion, so commonly met, that there is a special need to be on our guard against wishful thinking when we are considering this matter of Christian belief in God, often rests on a very serious misunderstanding of what the Christian teaching about God really is. It appears to be assumed that that teaching is merely of a comforting and comfortable kind—that it is such that we all of us ardently desire to believe it so soon as we understand it; therefore we must be especially on our guard against believing it too easily. Sometimes this view is part of a general theory which explains away all religious belief as being a fantasy, a fairy tale, which man elaborates out of his own mind in order to help himself along in a dangerous and difficult and disappointing world, even as a poor, downtrodden, frustrated kitchen maid helps herself along by reading "true confessions," or by imagining herself married to a millionaire. I have no hesitation in characterizing this theory as abysmally shallow and ignorant—if a thing can be both shallow and abysmal. A very superficial reading of the history of religion would show that belief in God, while it has brought comfort and strength, has also always carried with it to men's hearts a tremendous and inescapable demand, requiring, if need be, the surrender of life itself. It has confronted men with frightful choices and decisions and landed them in un-speakable martyrdoms. It has had in it the accent of judgment as well as of consolation.

Whatever may be true of religion in general, it is certainly not true of the Christian doctrine of God that, so soon as anyone understands it, he would so ardently and passionately desire to believe it that he would be in grave danger of being led astray by this desire. On the contrary, I suspect that a good deal of unbelief is due to the fact that people do not want to believe it, for fear of the demands it will make upon them, and that they run away from it even when its truth is laying hold upon them. In so far as that is so, it is clear that such folk are as much the victims of wishful thinking as anybody else; wishful thinking can work both ways. The Bible says, after all, that God is consuming fire just as much as it says he is refuge and strength; it talks about the wrath of God just as much as it talks about his love; it says that "it is a fearful thing to fall into the hands of the living God."

# CHAPTER II

# THE WORLD OF PERSONS

I HAVE spoken of the necessity for setting the Christian doctrine of God in an adequate context, if we are to think seriously and appropriately about it, and if its truth is to come home to us; we must be prepared to study large maps and take deep soundings.

Now there is one area of our life and experience which the Christian view firmly requires us to include in our universe of discourse, indeed, to put right at the center of the picture. This is what may be called "the world of persons"—the world of persons in relationship with one another. The Christian teaching about God and his relationship with man is personalistic through and through. That indeed, as already indicated, is to be our main theme throughout. Christianity says that whatever else may be true of God, and much else no doubt is true, it certainly is true that he is personal. And whatever else may be true of us as men, and much else no doubt is true, it certainly is true that God has created us persons and has set us in a world of personal relationship both to himself and to one another.

If I am asked at this stage what I mean by the words "personal" and "personal relationship," I must reply that it is not possible—and I believe not necessary—for me to say. I hope, indeed, that what I am going on to say later will help to give a richer content to these phrases, but I am bound to assume at the start that everybody knows in a general way what the words mean. We must assume that any man knows through his own self-awareness what it means to be a person, because he is one; and we must assume that he knows immediately through his relations with other human beings the difference between being treated as a person and being treated as a "non-person" or thing. In much the same way it would be no use talking about art to anybody who does not know—at least in a preliminary way—what you are referring to when you speak of beauty.

That Christianity should thus put a quite central emphasis on the world of persons seems to me to be at the outset one reason for asking and expecting people to treat it with respect and to consider gravely what it has to say. For nothing could be clearer than that our relationships to one another as persons do govern and control, for good or ill, almost everything else in our life—a glance at any newspaper shows that. Marriage and divorce; education; law, crime, and police; methods of government; relations of capital and labor; international relations and war; morale and leadership—in all these quite obviously *a* main question, and indeed quite often *the* main question, is what sort of relations human persons are setting up with one another or may be persuaded to set up with one another. But, indeed, there is no need to go to the newspapers. It is part of the most intimate texture of our daily life. Everyone in lodgings knows that the most important question is not, say, whether the bed is comfortable—

though I for one would not underrate the importance of that—but what sort of person the landlady is and what sort of personal relations can be established with her.

Obvious as all this seems to be, I think it is true to say that the modern mind, when it begins to think about the ultimate meaning of the strange universe in which we find ourselves alive, tends *not* to give this whole vast area of personal relationships the central and decisive place which it ought to have, and which the Christian view gives it. I suspect that this is one of the reasons why the Christian view and the thought of many of our contemporaries have got across one another and are out of tune with one another, so that they feel uncomfortable as soon as they hear that view expressed in unambiguous terms. The intense personalism of Christianity, which does not shrink from ascribing personal quality to God, vaguely puts them off; to entertain it at all requires from them, as it were, a stiff and noisy jerking of their mental machinery to another gear.

This is so strange in view of the actual situation of our lives that it is worth while inquiring what lies behind it. To do this will also bring to our notice some other important matters. We will consider in turn each of two forms of error into which our modern minds tend to fall in respect of this matter of the personal. The first is the tendency to ignore altogether the personal world as a clue to the nature of ultimate reality; the second is the tendency to bring it in, when it is brought in at all, in a form which fails to do justice to its distinctively personal quality—to bring it in, in such a way that it really ceases to be personal.

## I

First, then, the tendency to leave the personal realm out altogether in our thought about the ultimate nature of our world, our thought about God. Why do we do this? No doubt quite a number of reasons could be offered, but there is one reason which is worth dwelling on. It has to do with the simple fact that in seeking to get to know an object, it is the object we are interested in primarily; we are not interested in ourselves as interested in it, nor, certainly, in the mental processes by which we get to know it. Thus, when I look at an apple, it is the apple I see and not the eye with which I see it; nor do I see the nerves and nerve processes which transmit the retinal impression to the brain. And so it is right up to the highest reaches of our knowledge of the world about us. Our thought is an activity *of* ourselves, streaming outward from ourselves to a world which is not ourselves; but *ourselves,* as those who have the thoughts and do the thinking, we do not consider at all. We see the picture, but we are not ourselves in the picture. How could we be in it and see it at the same time?

Now this is not only the normal attitude of our minds, but the right attitude. Our powers of attention are limited, and if we attended to ourselves attending to the apple, we should miss the apple. But—this is the important point—it is the right attitude only so long as we are busy with getting to know of this, that, or the other bit

41

or part of our world; and it is, after all, as bits or parts that the world in the main does present itself to us for our everyday knowing and acting. If, however, we seek to reflect upon and to grasp the meaning and purpose of the world *as a whole*—and that is what we are doing when we think about God—then clearly this attitude, normal and proper elsewhere, will not do. Plainly, if we are going to look at and seek to know the world as a whole, we must no longer omit to notice ourselves as looking and knowing; for we, as looking and knowing, and knowing that we are looking and knowing—that is to say as persons—are certainly part of the world *taken as a whole*. The world taken as a whole cannot be merely the world about us; it must be the world which includes us.

This fact is obvious enough when it is pointed out, but it is persistently overlooked, especially by laboratory-trained minds. And it is overlooked precisely because of this ingrained habit whereby in getting to know a thing we omit all reference to the knower and to the process of knowing. It is only by an unusual and acrobatic effort that we can include these in the picture, like a dog trying to catch his own tail. How ingrained the habit is, is shown by the fact that we do not even notice the point when we observe other people looking out upon the world. One would think that we would see *them* as part of the world to be explained, but we do not. On the contrary, in our pondering upon the final meaning of things we vaguely picture the *whole* human race as standing over against the universe rather than as being integrally part of it and hence a major clue to its meaning. We picture humanity as a whole trying to figure things out, like a vast audience in a theater trying to puzzle out the meaning of a problem play; but we no more grasp the fact that its very endeavor to do this may be a major clue to the world's meaning than we think of the audience at the theater as being part of the play.

Let me give two examples of this tendency to omit the person who knows from the world which he seeks to know.

The first takes me back to my own student days; indeed, it played a part in my own mental history. When I was an undergraduate in Cambridge, Bertrand Russell published an essay which became famous at the time and is still sometimes referred to.[1] It was as magnificent in its language as it was complete in its pessimism. As one looks out upon the world—he said in effect—the conclusion is, to any honest mind, inevitable that it is all a soulless machine which cares nothing for man's dreams and ideals; therefore, there is nothing for man to do but proudly to preserve his own mind independent and intact in the midst of such an alien universe and, having flung down his challenge to it with something of the same contempt with which it apparently treats him, to bow at the end before its superior might and go down with dignity into the annihilation of death. Reading it as an undergraduate, I found it very impressive—we were very ready to be impressed by Russell in those days.

Then I read a reply from Pringle-Pattison, along a line which was at the time, and has been ever since, a check

---

[1] "The Free Man's Worship" (first published in 1903).

upon all my thought about these ultimate matters. The line was precisely the one which I have been indicating. The critic pointed out that Russell had fallen into the error, which so easily attends all our thought, of forgetting—or at least not giving anything like proper weight to—the fact that he himself as self-conscious personality, and mankind generally, is an integral part of the universe which he thus challenged and denounced so heartily. The universe had after all produced his mind and spirit, and other minds and spirits, with all their intense interior life, their powers of thought, their sense of personal dignity, their passion for ideals, their very capacity to rebel against such a world as Russell had come to conceive this to be. All this was, in effect, overlooked and treated as irrelevant, as though the universe were a drama and Russell merely a spectator who had mysteriously dropped in from outside. But the *person* called Russell, not to speak of other human persons, has not dropped in from outside; he has come forth from the world; he is part of what is going on; he is not a mere spectator. To ignore that fact, or to dismiss it as merely an impenetrable mystery telling us nothing of the final nature of things is, to say the least, a little arbitrary.

The second example is this: From the time of the Greek philosophers onward, the view has continually been put forward, in one form or another, that the whole universe is just a vast machine in which everything that happens is the necessary and predetermined result of what has gone before. Now, that there is such a rigidly mechanical aspect of events is obvious. It is obvious,

too, that this is very fortunate for persons such as we
are, for otherwise we could never live a personal life in
our world at all. It is only because the fire can be relied
on to boil the kettle, and sound-waves to carry our
speech, that we can indulge in that highly personal
activity called a tea party. One of our prime tasks is to
get to know what these mechanisms of our world are
and to use them; and natural science, of course, is just
the organized and systematic attempt to get to know
what they are.

But how comes it about that anybody should seriously
believe, and ask us to believe, that the whole world,
in all its spheres and in every aspect of every sphere, is
such a rigid mechanism? How comes it about that anybody should seriously believe, and ask us to believe,
that the whole of our personal life is but the absolutely
and inevitably predestined result of the play of blind
mechanical forces, so that even the most solemn and serious choice and decision must be regarded as the absolutely predetermined result of, say, conditioned reflexes,
or of the functioning of the endocrine glands, and no
more really a choice and decision than is the bursting
of a match into flame when it is rubbed?

There are problems and difficulties here with which
every member of even a junior philosophy class is familiar, and which I do not wish to minimize. The only
point I want at the moment to make concerns one reason
why such a view—running so counter to our sense of the
actual truth of things, and so utterly impossible to live by
in our personal dealings with one another—has neverthe-

less continually beguiled men's minds since the time
of the Greeks. The reason is, once again, that in the act
of thinking and knowing we do continually forget all
about the thinker and the knower himself, and particularly about this strange personal activity of thinking and
knowing. For if these theorists had thought about the
thinker and his act of thinking, it would surely have become clear to them that their theory cannot possibly be
true, for the reason that if it were true, then nobody could
ever know it to be true—the distinction between truth and
falsehood would in fact vanish altogether.

That sounds perhaps somewhat abstruse, but it is
really quite simple. Let us suppose that you, as a holder
of this theory, say to me, who am a denier of it, that my
thoughts are the mechanically necessary resultant of
say, my physiological make-up. I am then bound to
retort, and you are bound to admit, that your thoughts
—including your thought about this theory—are equally
the necessary resultant of *your* physiological make-up;
and since that is the case with all our thoughts, what is
the use of arguing? If your glands necessarily produce a
mechanistic theory, and my glands necessarily produce
a nonmechanistic theory, then notions of truth and
falsity, or of setting ourselves to find the one and avoid
the other, do not apply; for in each case glands and
theory are just facts absolutely on a level, as natural
and inevitable as one another, and notions of logic and
truth are out of place. No, the only thing for you to do
is to give me a dose of medicine, and see to it that I do
not give you a dose of medicine first—just as, I am told,

in administering a pill to a horse through a blowpipe it is as well to see that the horse does not blow first.

But of course the thing is ridiculous. The whole world of truth and reason and knowledge and personal co-operation in search of truth is reduced to complete non-sense by an all-inclusive mechanistic theory—including the mechanistic theory itself—and the only reason why that has so often been overlooked is precisely that the personal knower and his act of knowing are overlooked.[2]

## II

The second and more important of the two errors into which modern thought tends to fall is that, even when it does turn its attention to the world of persons, it fails to do justice to its distinctively personal quality.

It would be absurd to suggest that modern systematic thought is not interested in any way at all in persons and their relationships to one another; the sciences of psychology, sociology, economics, and history, all have to do with persons and their relationship to one another, and they are very important and valuable studies. They are all the rage, too. But they *are* sciences, and that is their limitation in respect of this matter of grasping the distinctive nature of the personal world. They cover a certain amount of the facts, but they do not, and cannot, cover them all; and what they do not and

[2] The point is familiar to every student of philosophy. But, alas, so few study philosophy. Quite recently I met a brilliant young law student from Guatemala who vigorously professed this all-inclusive mechanistic view. He said he had given up his Christian faith because of it. I put the point set forth to him, and he frankly confessed it had never struck him. In this he was typical.

cannot cover is precisely that which does differentiate this personal sphere from other spheres—that which makes it necessary to explore it, if it is to be known at all, by a different method. Yet so many people, in their obsession with laboratory science, do not see this and so they fail to give the personal world its due place in their interpretation of the world.

In order to make plain what I have in mind, let us imagine that I am a scientist working alone all day in my laboratory at, say, the digestive processes of earthworms, and then going home to my wife and family, with whom I stand in a deeply personal relationship of love and trust. Is it not clear that in stepping from the scientific laboratory into my home I do step almost literally from one world to another, so profound is the change in the type of relationship into which I enter with the realities with which I am dealing?

Thus, first, as a scientist in the laboratory, the one thing I try to get away from all the time is the concrete, particular, individual, unrepeatable object; and the one thing I want to get *to* is a generalization, no matter how abstract, which shall be true of all objects whatsoever of the type I am studying. It is true that I can study only one particular earthworm at a time, or at most a small collection of earthworms; but I am interested in a single earthworm only in so far as it can be treated as a "case," an example of all earthworms whatsoever. If I lose or spoil one earthworm, I can at once put another in its place with nothing lost except time. Indeed, to get interested in an individual earthworm as such, assuming that an earthworm has any individuality to get interested in —which it has not—would be a distraction and a hindrance to my work. As a scientist I am interested only in events, or aspects of events, that recur, for my task as a scientist is to make generalizations. I am certainly not in a position to say that there are no events which happen only once; all I can say is that if there are such events, I am not, as a scientist, interested in them.

But, on the other hand, when I get into my home, the one thing I *am* interested in, that I clamor for, that I delight in discovering and hold onto in the persons with whom I have the distinctively personal relationship of love and trust, is their individuality—all that makes each one of them his own unique, unrepeatable, distinctive, irreplaceable self. My supreme interest here is in events which happen only once. Personal friendship, love to persons, always thus individualizes, flees from the merely class generalization. It is true that in all kinds of ways a human person can be generalized about, can be put in a class; indeed, it may sometimes be most necessary and helpful so to do—as, for example, when the doctor comes and treats my quite "unrepeatable" wife as one case of common, and all too frequently repeated, cold in the head. No one would deny that the generalizing activity of science has a place in relation to person. But that only serves to stress the point I am making, namely, that the place where the applicability of science ends is the place where distinctively personal relations begin. The mark of the latter is precisely this central emphasis on individuality, and utter recoil from the merely class generalization. It is this highly individualizing interest, which arises as soon as we begin to grasp persons as persons and to love and trust them as persons, that helps to make death and bereavement the distressing things they are in human life. An earthworm is replaceable; a person is not.

Then, second, there is another difference more difficult to express. In the laboratory, dealing with my earthworms, my microscope, my reagents of various sorts, I am, so far as my own will is concerned, in a very real sense a dictator; I am "monarch of all I survey." There is of course a sense in which, if I am to be successful in my scientific inquiry, I must submit myself to the facts; I must, if you like, let them dictate to me. I cannot will earthworm, microscope, and reagents to be other than they are, in order to save myself trouble or to help my theories; but that is beside the point. The point is that my will is the only will at work in the situation. Within the limits set by the facts I am undisputed master. I manipulate things as I wish, and my hope is that as I discover more and more generalizations about them I shall be able to manipulate them even more effectively in the interests of my own purposes. I do not ask the earthworm's permission to put him under the microscope; there is no permission to ask.

But when I step into my home among persons, I am in a different world. Why? Because my will now undergoes a new and altogether different check or limitation, the limitation of meeting other intelligent, self-directing, self-conscious, *personal* wills besides my own. The will of another person confronts me with an independent and inaccessible source of activity which I know I am not able, and ought not to try, to manipulate and control into an instrument of my own will; and the other person himself knows that I cannot and ought not to do so. I may, in fact, in my egotism, and perhaps in some measure through force of the habits I have acquired in dealing with earthworms in the laboratory, try to do so. I may, in the manner which used to be ascribed—probably quite unjustly—to the Victorian papa, stand with my back to the fire and order people about. But the extent to which I can do that is very limited. Rebellion is always just around the corner, and a repressed and smoldering resentment is not even around the corner; people sense it as soon as they come into the house. For in so behaving I am treating the personal world as something other than it really is; in fact, I am not treating it as personal at all. I am running as directly counter to reality as I would be if in the laboratory I took the opposite line and addressed personal requests to my earthworm, instead of taking him between finger and thumb and just putting him where I want him to be.

I spoke a moment ago of another will's acting as a check and limitation to my own; but, indeed, in proportion as the highly personal relationship of love and trust is present, it is not felt as a limitation at all. I do not desire to manipulate a person when I really apprehend him as a person. I rejoice in his independence, and most of all I rejoice when a harmony of trust and co-operation is achieved in and through his independence and mine.

Third, I have more than once spoken of trust as a distinctively personal relationship. Now there is also an aspect of my work in the laboratory which might not inappropriately be called trust. As a scientist I am indeed an extraordinarily trustful and believing person, though I am not usually very conscious of it. I believe, for example, that the world has a fixed and settled order, which will not change over night. I believe that that order is capable of being grasped by the human reason and amenable to human control. I believe that the behavior of the objects with which I am dealing can be firmly relied upon—that this behavior will repeat itself in a completely predictable and reliable way.

This believing trust of the scientist is worth noting—for he is sometimes pictured as the very incarnation of hesitant and cautious questioning, never going an inch beyond what the facts warrant; but he is really full of belief and trust. The scientist does not notice it because, as I said earlier, he so seldom notices the knower and the knowing process. It would be interesting to inquire what is the source of this trust and what is its justification, and what it implies; but at the moment we think only of the scientist's confidence in the future regular behavior of the objects with which he is dealing. What is the basis of that particular confidence? It is plainly the belief, continually verified in practice, that such objects are *mechanically necessitated* to act as they do, the belief that they act, and will act, in strict proportion to the external environmental forces that play upon them.

Now observe, once again, what happens when I step

into my home. This is very important in relation to what I shall go on to say later. Here again something which we call trust is central and dominant; I trust my wife, I trust my friends, I have confidence as to their future behavior. But what is the basis of this confidence in the home? It is the exact opposite of the basis of my confidence in the laboratory. The basis in the laboratory is that the objects with which I am dealing are mechanically necessitated by the forces that play upon them; the basis in the home is precisely that they are *not*—so wide, so very wide, is the gulf between the world of things and the world of persons. Plainly, if I thought that my wife were mechanically necessitated in her behavior by every force that plays upon her, I could never trust her out of my sight. For I could never be sure that forces other and stronger than those which now play upon her, when she is within my sight, would not become operative and re-direct all her conduct into another channel; I could never be sure that, like the weathercock, she would not turn with every wind that blows.

And note this: If I have to deal with a man whom I cannot trust because he *is* in greater or less degree at the mercy of the external environmental forces which play upon him, all I can do is to bring my own compelling pressures to bear upon him. I have to try to manipulate his situation, or play upon his fears with a threat, or upon his cupidity with a bribe, or upon his credulity with a lie, or upon his body with a fetter or a prison cell. In short, I have to treat him as a thing. I have no option, for I must have some basis for action, and if I cannot trust him in the nonmechanical sense, that is, as a person, I must endeavor to trust him in the mechanical sense, that is, as a thing—though even then I can never achieve anything like the surety which I have in relation to a friend; the man who gives bribes is always at the mercy of the man who can give a bigger one.

I think I have said enough now in support of the point I am making. The point is that there is a certain profound disparity between the world in which science moves, and the methods it uses, and the world in which we live our lives as persons along with other persons, especially when we live them on what would universally be recognized as the highest level of distinctively personal relationship. And one result of this disparity, assisted by the tendency to forget the knower in the act of knowing, is apt to be a certain initial bias against, and discomfort in the presence of, the intense personalism of the Christian view of the world. It is vaguely felt that such personalism is not "scientific," and some people today seem to fear being accused of that almost as much as in an earlier period they feared being accused of witchcraft.

This bias must be got rid of if a man is going to make anything of the Christian view of life at all; and in view of what I have said, it ought not to be difficult to get rid of it. The personal world *is* radically different from the thing world, and it is the world we live in most of our days, and in which most of our major problems are centered. The assertion of Christianity that the key to the final meaning of our life is to be found in the personal world is therefore far from being the intrinsically improbable or incredible thing that some modern minds find it to be, nor is its invitation to live in that world and to explore it under its guidance lightly to be set on one side.

## III

We must now consider a further aspect of this world of persons in relationship; for until we have grasped it, we cannot understand the Christian view or be persuaded of its essential truth.

Let us go back to the second of the three points of difference which we have just set forth, between our attitude to the objects with which we deal in the scientific laboratory and our attitude to the persons with whom we deal when we step into the distinctively personal world. The point was that in the laboratory I am, so far as the exercise of my will is concerned, a dictator. Within the limits set by the facts and by my own knowledge or ignorance of them, I am undisputed master. But when I step into my home, my will undergoes another and altogether different check or limitation—the limitation of encountering other intelligent, self-directing, self-conscious wills besides my own. In the will of another person my will is confronted with an independent and inaccessible source of activity—a source of activity which, so far as we are in one situation together, I must take into account; but which I must not, and indeed for the most part cannot, merely manipulate and control into a passive instrument of my own purposes. In so far as I try to do that, and still more if I succeed, I reduce him from the status of a person to the status of a thing; and the same applies of course to his relationship to me in the situation in which we are both involved.

We have then this strange state of affairs, the strangeness of which is only veiled from us by its everyday familiarity: that two independent sources of activity, neither of which is accessible to, or controllable by, the other, are nevertheless indissolubly bound up with one another, condition one another, and cannot escape one another; they are free of one another, and yet bound to one another. That, I suggest, is the very heart and essence of the personal world, of any situation in which two or more persons are involved; the persons are bound to one another by their common situation, yet free of one another —dependent on one another, yet independent of one another. Each limits and conditions the other; yet each is free of the other.

That being how things are, it may well be asked: How can two wills, two persons, ever come into unity and harmony with one another? How can they ever achieve that unity and harmony which we recognize as quite indispensable to any satisfactory living together, and as finding its highest expression in the loyalty and trust which are characteristic of, say, a happy home life? The attempt to achieve harmony by the tyrannical domination of one will by another, we have seen, merely frustrates itself; it is a running away from the problem, from the distinctively personal realm. The answer to this question—How are unity and harmony of a truly personal kind to be achieved?—confronts us with something very fundamental to the Christian understanding of these matters.

This is the notion, or rather the fact, of "claim." Harmony between human persons becomes possible only when each, as he confronts the other, recognizes himself to be under a certain constraint—the constraint of what we call a claim: the other has claims upon me, I have claims upon the other. A moment's thought will make plain how peculiar to the personal world this notion of claim is. We do not and cannot think of things—the earthworm, the microscope, the table—as making claims upon us. But persons do. As soon as I become aware of them in their distinctive nature as personal, I become aware of claim. If I recognize the claim, I acknowledge them as persons. If I do not recognize it or, recognizing it, disregard it, I put them for the moment into the class of things. Incidentally it is worth remarking that by failing to recognize it I put myself in the class of things also. For if it is the mark of a person to confront me with a claim, it is equally the mark of my being a person that I should recognize myself to be under the claim. A one-hundred-per-cent dictator, if such a being could ever exist, would not be a person. He would simply be a peculiar source of overriding energy, strictly comparable to a gale or a man-eating tiger. Even Hitler had to preserve a semblance of humanity by speaking of the claim of Germans upon him, as well as of his claim upon Germans.[3]

[3] Cf. Berdyaev, *Slavery and Freedom* (1943), p. 61: "The enslaving of another is also the enslaving of oneself. . . . The master is not a personality, just as the slave is not a personality."

If I am asked to say more precisely what I mean by "claim," I do not know that I can do so, any more than I can say what I mean when I speak of having a sensation of red. It is an ultimate of the personal world, just as red is an ultimate of the sensory world, not to be expressed in terms of anything else. You, being a person in the personal world, know what it is. If you do not know what it is, then I know of no means of telling you. I think, however, it is not difficult to see that in this notion of claim the two apparently contrary notions—of persons being bound to one another and yet being in another sense free of one another—are brought together.

A claim, as I have put it elsewhere,[4] is a relationship between two personal wills of such a kind that each is conditioned by the other yet each remains free of the other. I am always free to reject your claim upon me, otherwise it would not be claim, but compulsion; but I am inescapably conditioned by it, for my acceptance or rejection of it becomes instantly, and possibly fatefully, part of the course of events, part of my history and yours. It does this because the relationship of claim-upon-one-another is part of the essential constitution and structure of the personal world, and nothing can alter it—just as gravity is part of the essential constitution and structure of the physical world. It is no more possible to ignore the one with impunity than it is to ignore the other.

It is clear, however, that in this mutual conditioning of two persons by one another through claim we have only the raw material, so to speak, of that unified, har-

[4] *The Servant of the Word* (1941), p. 42.

monious world of loyalty and trust and co-operation which persons can build up with one another—which, indeed, they must build up with one another if they are not to be continually falling foul of the actual constitution of the personal world and degrading one another into the status of things. Claims, or what are taken to be claims, may, as we all know, clash with one another. This may be due to the complexity of the situation in which persons find themselves involved; or to the fact that men disagree with one another as to what the rightful claims of persons are; or, more often, to the fact that into the sphere of claim there continually intrudes the clamor—to use a significant variation of the same root—of powerful instincts or of an ingrained self-regard.

How then is a unity of loyalty and trust ever to be built up? Part, at least, of the answer is that there is no way in which it can permanently be done other than by persons acknowledging themselves to be, in their reciprocal claims, under a third and higher claim, which comprehends their claims upon one another and lays itself equally and impartially upon all in an absolute rule, the right of which to undeviating obedience neither questions. If you and I, as we deal with one another, both acknowledge ourselves to be under one and the same higher, more comprehensive, and overriding claim, that fact at once brings our claims on one another into the same world. It puts them under the same checks, the same criteria of judgments, no matter how much they may apparently and incidentally diverge from one another; and an indispensable basis of unity is established, even though many difficult problems will still have to be solved and adjustments made.

It is easy to see the relation of this to the building up of trust between persons. To mention only one point: I spoke earlier of the difference between the trust which I exercise in the laboratory and the trust which I exercise in my home—in the laboratory I trust the behavior of things because they are rigidly controlled by the forces which play upon them; in my home I trust persons to the degree in which I can be sure they are not. How then can I be sure of anyone that he will *not* at any moment fall victim to environmental compulsions that play upon him? How can I ever come to trust him? Well, I suppose I can never be absolutely sure; but I have a very firm basis of assurance, the firmest that is possible in the free personal world, when I know that the person with whom I am dealing recognizes himself to be under an absolute claim —a claim which he accepts as requiring his undeviating obedience no matter how fiercely environmental stimuli may be stinging him into this or that activity, a claim requiring his obedience at any cost, even, if need be, at the cost of life itself. And only along the same lines can he be sure of me—only when we both recognize an absolute claim of some sort, which we acknowledge we must obey at any cost, are we both on the way to being released from the play of environmental forces upon our instinctive and animal natures. And if we both acknowledge the *same* absolute claim as governing our claims upon one another, then a deep, rich unity in freedom becomes at last a possibility.

This can be well illustrated by the marriage relationship. In marriage you have a relationship between persons which on the one hand, if it is to reach a point of real stability and happiness, must include the completest possible mutual trust, and on the other hand involves powerful instincts and wants which are peculiarly liable to be at the mercy of environmental excitement. How wise, therefore, are those who put and keep their married relationship under a vow—a vow made not merely to one another, but also to a higher will that claims them both absolutely in and through their claim for loyalty to one another. The marriage vow, therefore, is *not* a limitation and bondage; on the contrary, it is the way out of bondage, the escape from an impersonal bondage to the chance excitements of the world and particularly to the imperious instincts of sex. It is not merely a chivalrous romanticism, but rather a deep insight into the personal world which says:

> I could not love thee, Dear, so much,
> Lov'd I not Honour more.

## IV

In all this we have not yet said anything that could be regarded as distinctively Christian, in the sense that only a Christian believer could be expected to accept it. Not a few serious minds today recognize—for, indeed, it would seem to be obvious enough—that what humanity needs above all things else is that men and nations should find the way of living in harmony together, and that such harmony is realizable only on the basis of a common and loyal acknowledgment of a universal standard of values which lays its claims equally and absolutely upon all. The distinctively Christian understanding of the personal world comes into view in respect of two further fundamental points.

The first concerns the source of this higher claim, in the acknowledgment of which alone human relations can be built up into a harmony of loyalty and trust. The Christian faith can never be wholly satisfied with saying "loved I not *Honour* more"; it insists rather on saying "loved I not *God* more." It insists, that is to say, that the source of the higher claim which comprehends all other claims is the will of the infinite personal God, and that only in the knowledge of, and right response to, this is the harmony of human life possible. In other words, every finite person—by the very nature and constitution of the personal world as God has made it—stands in a dual *personal* relationship of claim: he is related at the same time and all the time to the claim of the infinite Person and to the claim of other finite persons. It is important to grasp that it is a *dual* relationship in which he stands, and not two relationships. It is one relationship with, as it were, two poles—the claim of God and the claim of the neighbor. The two claims are distinguishable in thought, but in actuality wholly inseparable from one another. The claim of my neighbor is always part of God's claim on me. God's claim on me meets me always in and through the claim of my neighbor.

These truths find concrete expression and illustration in our Lord's teaching that it is no use worshiping God when we are in a state of enmity with one another, or asking the forgiveness of God when we refuse to forgive one another, or expecting acquittal at the judgment seat of God when we ignore the claim of a thirsty man for a cup of cold water. And, most impressively of all, they find expression in the words he puts into the mouth of God—words which might well make us tremble if we really believed them or were not so familiar with them: "Inasmuch as ye did it not to one of the least of these, ye did it not to me." In such words there comes to expression, not a piece of romantic sentimentalism, but a very profound and challenging philosophy of personal relationships.

The second fundamental truth in the distinctively Christian view I shall at this point do no more than mention. It concerns the question of what the content of the divine-human claim is, and how, amid the darkness and perplexity and corruption of our human personal life, we may apprehend it and respond to it. According to the Christian faith, the answer to these questions has been given once and for all by the divine Person himself, in a great act of self-disclosure in Christ.

I shall speak further on these two points in the next two chapters. Meanwhile I would like to emphasize once again, particularly in respect of the first of them, what I have called the radical personalism of the Christian viewpoint. At no point in its revelation of the ultimate realities which underlie and environ human existence will it allow us to pass into an impersonalized world. It is precisely at this point that many of our more serious-minded contemporaries, to whom reference was made a minute ago, part company with it. Recognizing the need for a universal standard of moral values which lays its claims authoritatively and equally upon all, they nevertheless refuse to think of such a standard in terms of a higher personal Will. Like the poet just quoted, they will speak only of honor. They will speak of the moral law, or of ideal values or essences, or of the concrete universal of "Good," [5] but not of the righteous will of the personal God which makes its claims upon us. It would take us too far aside from our main purpose to enter upon a full discussion of this type of view. I wish only to make two comments in line with the principle laid down in the last chapter that in our thought about God it is necessary to take deep soundings and study large maps.

First, I would ask those who take this view to consider whether, in their acknowledgment of the claim of higher or universal values, or whatever they may be called, to the allegiance of their wills, there is not in fact an implicit reference of the claim to an ultimate will and purpose of righteousness. I do not mean logically implicit, but implicit in the sense that the reference to a higher will as the source of the claim really is an integral part of their awareness even though it is not brought explicitly before the mind, and even though they are minded in any case, for various theoretical reasons, to deny its validity in advance. To put it differently, does not the awareness of claim in its full impact on a serious nature carry within it, even though in a dim and disguised form, a reference to a personal Reality who claims? Ultimately each must answer

[5] As Miss Wodehouse, in her beautiful book, *One Kind of Religion* (1944).

this question for himself. I am only pleading that it should be asked, and asked again and again, and that in these critical matters we should take care not to remain too much in the shallow places of our nature. Certainly the obligation is on us all the time to try to come to an ever clearer awareness of the real nature of our deepest convictions. A writer like Hartmann ought to take more note of the fact that in his efforts to do justice to the moral consciousness he is continually compelled to ascribe personal qualities to what he calls timeless moral essences or values.[6]

Second, I would suggest that a wider review of the actual moral situation of mankind might well raise a demurrer in any man's mind as to the adequacy of the view we are commenting on and call for its fresh examination. There can be no denying that the human situation is in very great measure one of the direst need and helplessness. It is all very well to speak in solemn terms of the claim of higher values upon us all, and of the urgent necessity to recognize it, but what has that to say to the man who has brought his life, and the lives of others, to a bog of moral filth and impotence; or has lost a child just blossoming into the fullness of personal life—perhaps seen it murdered or tortured or raped in a concentration camp; or who has found every good cause, to which, in heroic response to higher values, he has set his hand, go down in ruin—not to speak of other things in the full tale of human corruption and anguish? There is little or no succor for men in this view, and one cannot help

[6] See, for example, his *Ethics* (Eng. tr. 1932), Vol I, chap. xvii.

suspecting sometimes that those who hold it have lived a very sheltered and cushioned existence, or else have managed to combine with a great concern for higher values a certain toughness of fiber in relation to the muck and misery which characterize so much in human life.

But has Christianity anything to say in answer to these ills of suffering humanity? We believe it has, and we are to try to set forth some aspects of its answer in what follows. But it is an answer which it *cannot give apart from the initial insistence that the personal world is one which includes the infinite personal God as well as the finite persons of men and women.* All these things—the deep need of humanity, the Christian message in relation to it, the initial insistence on the personal God—must be taken together if the truth of Christianity is to be brought home to men. In other words, it is very necessary that the Christian message should be apprehended in its full range and depth before the solemn decision is made to set it on one side.

I have spoken of "claim" as being integral to the personal world, and of the reciprocal recognition of "claim" as being essential to the right ordering of that world. I am called upon to acknowledge your claims upon me and you to acknowledge mine upon you. It may be asked, How far is it necessary for me to be aware of, and even to assert, my own rightful claims upon you? Obviously, in so far as my rightful claims as a person are recognized by you, there will be no need for me to be explicitly aware of them, still less to assert them. That is the situation in a relationship of real mutual trust and love. But if you do not recognize them, or if you ignore them, and so do not treat me as a person, it will be improper for me to ignore the wrongness of that relationship and to act as though it were otherwise. I am not called upon to acquiesce in being treated as a thing and not as a person.

Everything depends, however, on the way in which my own claim as a person is put forward. In so far as the protest is a manifestation of a narrowly egotistic self-regard, it will achieve little or nothing in the way of establishing right relations. But if it is a genuine expression of concern for the building up of right personal relations *generally*—that is to say, if it expresses a recognition (*a*) of the claims of all persons whatsoever upon both of us and upon all men, (*b*) of the claim of God upon all men in and through their claims upon one another, (*c*) of the claim upon me of this one person who is misusing me, so that it may be said that he, as it were, is entitled, or has a claim, to the protest I make—then the situation is obviously very different and may have a very different issue. The trouble is, of course, that so much egotistic self-regard, so much of our own ignoring of the other's claims, always *is* mixed up in our protests and rebukes, and that the other man usually knows it.

A more difficult question, arising out of the analysis of the personal order which we have given, is whether, seeing that human persons stand in a personal relationship to God, they may be said to stand in a relationship of claim upon him. This is a thought from which the sensitive religious mind instantly and rightly recoils. The answer would seem to be that, while a human being by virtue of his being a person may be said, in a sense, to *have* a claim upon God, nevertheless it can never be right for him ever to come before God *making* a claim upon him.

The sense in which a human being may be said to have a claim upon God is this: Inasmuch as God has created us persons and set us in an order of personal relationship to himself, he will, in all his dealings with us, respect the personal status which he has bestowed. That is to say, he will respect our claim as persons, for otherwise he would stultify his own purpose. In creating a person he creates a being with claims upon himself, and in honoring those claims he does no more than recognize his own handiwork and remain consistent with his own purpose. Thus, as we shall see later, God always respects human freedom. In so doing he respects the claim of the personal status he has himself bestowed.[7]

On the other hand, as the Christian mind rightly feels, the relationship between the human person and the divine person is such that it can never be right for a man to come before God asserting claims, for two reasons. First, because the human person, if he is rightly apprehending God, cannot possibly forget that he has come into being, and is maintained in being, as a person, only because of God's creative will. Obviously it would be nonsense to speak of a human person's having a claim to exist as a person prior to his being given existence as a person. This primordial relationship of utter and, so to say, claimless creatureliness and dependence, in the deeply religious mind, engulfs, as it were, the claims of being a person

[7] See Chap. VI.

which are part of the bestowed character of his creaturely existence. Second, if a man entertains the thought that he must assert his claims as a person in the presence of God, then that merely reveals that he is not apprehending God as he really is; for, according to the Christian revelation, God in his relations with persons, is utter righteousness and love and therefore unfailingly honors the claims of the persons whom he has made. In other words, the man who feels he must assert claims to God is still in darkness. He is "alienated from the life of God" and needs above all the light of Christ.

# CHAPTER III

# MAN THE SINNER

WE SAID in the last chapter that Christianity puts the personal world at the center of its view of life and insists that it shall be interpreted in a way that does full justice to its distinctive nature as personal. Seeking thus to interpret it, we found at its heart the quite distinctively personal relationship we call "claim"—God's absolute claim on men meeting them in and through their claim on one another, their claim on one another being always part of, included in, God's claim on them all. We shall now pursue this subject further and set forth some other aspects of the Christian understanding of man, particularly of man as sinful.

In presenting the Christian view of man as sinful to our more serious contemporaries, we are today in at least an initially more advantageous position than was the case when some of us were younger. For the judgment that something is very radically wrong with human life can hardly be dismissed any longer as the outcome of the morbid pessimism of Christian orthodoxy. Today such a judgment hardly amounts to more than an empirical report of facts open for all to see. Nor do the many fine things in human life—courage, self-sacrifice, devotion to duty—in any way alter the judgment; on the contrary, they underscore it. For if man were all devilry, there would be no reason to suppose that anything had *gone* wrong; indeed, being men ourselves, we should not be able to recognize devilry as devilry. It is only because man has such grand capacities, including the capacity to recognize devilry as devilry, and yet continues in varying degrees to do devilish things and to make a foul mess of his life that we are compelled to conclude that something has gone wrong.

It is obvious that the Christian view of what is wrong with man must rest upon the Christian view of what man essentially is, independently of his wrongness—what he would be if nothing were wrong. A former colleague of mine used always to ask his elementary class in philosophy to write an essay on the "doorknobity of the doorknob"—that which makes a certain object a true, "essential" doorknob distinguishable from any other knob, say the knob on the banisters. So also, if we are to be told what is wrong with man, we must first be told what "true and proper" man is; we must first understand what essentially is "the humanity of the human," what is the essential secret of human nature as distinct from that of any other sort of living creature.

I think we can perhaps most usefully make plain the Christian view of the essence of man by setting it in contrast with other views which in variant forms are current today. This will not only throw into greater relief the Christian view but also prepare the way for some of the things I want to say at the end of this chapter. To describe these other views in a few sentences, as I am going to do, will give them a sharpness of definition which they do not in reality possess in the minds of those who are influenced by them, but that may be an advantage, for it is their very vagueness which makes them so dangerous. Probably we are all influenced by some, or even all, of them in some degree.

# I

There is first what may perhaps be called the purely *naturalistic* view of men. According to this view man is not *essentially* different from any other member of the animal kingdom. Any distinctive qualities he may possess have emerged in the universal struggle for existence, and have no significance other than their usefulness in relation to that struggle. No doubt some of these qualities are very remarkable, or at least they seem so to man himself; still, they have been developed in exactly the same way as have the qualities of, say, the beaver or the bee—equally remarkable in their own way. They have been developed, that is to say, in order to subserve the fundamental biological instincts and urges, such as hunger and sex. Along with this view there goes a more or less deterministic view of human behavior. Men are what they are and behave as they do simply because of the interplay of the instincts and urges just referred to, as these function under the influence of heredity, education, social pressures, diet, glands, and so forth. A human being is just a highly complex meeting place for forces and influences which play upon him, mold, manipulate, and stimulate him, like any other animal.

It is important to realize that this sort of view does in

fact underlie much of men's treatment of one another, even when a naturalistic determinism as an all-inclusive theory of human behavior is not explicitly accepted, or even considered. As was said in the preceding chapter, we are always trying to manipulate people, as though they were so much plastic material to be conditioned and controlled by cunningly applied stimuli of various sorts. This is a view of man which clearly enters quite considerably into Marxian communism, into fascism, and, more subtly, into the tone and temper of modern industrial capitalism. Equally clearly it enters into the whole business of propaganda, and into much advertising, for propaganda and advertising are often little more than an elaborate process of conditioning the dog to beg.

There is, of course, some truth in the view; if there were not, it would have no plausibility at all. There is a sense in which man is just an animal among animals, a product of the struggle for existence; and certainly he is to a considerable degree deterministically conditioned and conditionable. It *is* possible to get at and to control men through animal needs and instincts; it *is* possible to fashion them by bringing all sorts of influences to bear upon the excitabilities, the plasticities, of their nature; but is this all the truth about a human being? Is it the most important, the *essential,* truth? Christianity, of course, says emphatically No.

Second, there is a view which is in some ways the exact opposite of the one just described, though one not infrequently observes it occupying the same muddled mind at different times. This view distinguishes and isolates man

73

from the rest of the animal world—even though in other
ways he obviously is an animal—in that he is able to seek,
to be interested in, and to enjoy what are vaguely called
higher, spiritual, or cultural, values. Herein is the essential
secret of man's being, the task which is set him by his
distinctive nature, and in the fulfillment of which the true
maturity of his being can be realized—the progressive
enthronement of cultural values. This view might be
called the *cultural* or, if you like, the high-brow view of
human nature. The higher your brow becomes, the more
cultured you are, the more you are at home with the
highest, or at least the most recent, products of art, drama,
music, literature—the more of a "pukka" human being
you are, the more the essence of humanity has come to its
finest flower in you. Along with this view there usually
goes an optimistic conviction that human life generally—
by means of better education and proper social arrangements, aided by science, psychology, and possibly eugenics
—can be made and will be made a veritable temple of
truth and beauty.

> These things shall be: a loftier race
>     Than e'er the world hath known shall rise,
> With flame of freedom in their souls
>     And light of knowledge in their eyes.
>
> They shall be gentle, brave, and strong
>     To spill no drop of blood, but dare
> All that may plant man's lordship firm
>     On earth, and fire, and sea, and air.

# MAN THE SINNER

New arts shall bloom of loftier mould,
  And mightier music thrill the skies,
And every life shall be a song,
  When all the earth is paradise.[1]

I do not doubt this sort of view also *is* in most of our minds—perhaps far more than we know. How often, as I listened to Bach or Beethoven at a symphony concert, have I caught myself feeling that somehow I was helping human life to be what it is meant to be—really helping things along, far more than the low-brows who are at the variety show around the corner. And, once again, there *is* truth in this view. There *are* wonderful powers in man. Especially wonderful are his powers of creativeness in art and music and drama; but is it the whole truth—is it, or does it come near, the essential truth? Christianity says emphatically No. And experience also, I think, says No. Hitler, we are told, loved Wagner, and Nero is said to have played the fiddle while Rome burned. I do not doubt he played it very well.

A third view which is abroad today is difficult to describe, partly because it is extremely vague; but it is none the less real for that. It might be called the *vitalist* view. It is in part a reaction against the last view, with its tendency to a thin and polished intellectualism, its call for a schooling of the passions in the interest of what most people are ready to think of as a somewhat remote and academic high-brow culture. Life, it is said, is deeper and richer than these pallid abstractions called spiritual values

[1] John Addington Symonds.

75

can comprehend. It includes also the immediacies of the passional and even the physical side of our natures. "Life" with a capital L, that is the ruling category, Life to be lived to the full here and now. Let us accept ourselves as the mysterious life force which throbs through all sentient existence has made us—vital organisms with, be it always remembered, bodily and sensory as well as intellectual processes—and as such let us *be* ourselves and express ourselves.

All very vague and woolly no doubt, but easily recognizable by anyone who is at all sensitive to contemporary currents of thought. The most extreme and obvious expression of it has been the Nazi movement in Germany, with its suspicion of the intellectuals, its repudiation of the whole classic tradition of universal culture and values, its insistence that one thinks with one's blood, its reversion to pagan nature gods, its worship of the "Leader," in whose intuitions the mysterious life force which surges through the German *Volk,* and in other ways through all history, finds articulate expression.

And once again we observe there is truth in this view. It does endeavor to take note of at least some of the facts of our nature. Man is body as well as mind, or rather he is body-mind, neither to be separated from the other; he is flesh as well as spirit, passional as well as cultural, instinctive and sensual as well as rational and intellectual; and the little daylight patch of his fully conscious awareness is carried all the time on subconscious "deeps" whose impulses and activities are infinitely more mysterious and incalculable than we realize or perhaps, in our flat, bourgeois, conventional morality, are ready to admit. But is it the whole truth? Is it, or does it come near, the essential truth? Christianity says emphatically No.

There is a fourth view which is perhaps only a variant of the last view, but it is worth stating separately. It may be called the *group* or *collectivist* view; or taking account of its most obvious contemporary form, the *nationalistic* view. What this view says in effect is that the essential meaning of human life is not to be found in the individual; it is to be comprehended only in terms of the social group to which the individual belongs. Man is what he is only because of the race, or the *Volk,* or the nation, to which he belongs. He has no standing apart from this, and no significance except as one in whom the distinctive life of his nation temporarily dwells as an organ of its ongoing history and destiny.

We misunderstand ourselves, and we misunderstand the modern world, if we dismiss this sort of thing as a silly jingoism fit only for docile Germans or fervid Japanese with morbid inferiority feelings. The cult of the nation, the tendency to let our best and most heroic desires and aspirations come to a sort of final resting point in the service, the preservation, the prosperity, the good name of our own country, is in most of us; and during war it undergoes a most powerful reinforcement. It is the more seductive because it can and does carry men to the final sacrifice of life, and because it can so easily attach to itself the august name of God and so make itself appear a far less narrowly nationalistic and group concern than it really is. "Sweet and fitting it is to die for one's country." A letter from a young airman killed in action was published in England during the war just ended, and it was in many ways a most noble and moving letter; but it contained these words, "One thing can never be altered. I shall have lived and died an Englishman. *Nothing else matters one jot.*" [2]

And, of course, once again, there is truth in this view. We are what we are because of our national tradition and heritage; our life is inseparable from that of our group; our happiness and well-being depend on its happiness and well-being. We are all of us incurably and utterly American or British or whatever it may be, down to the innermost core of our being. But is it the whole truth? Is it, or does it come near, the essential truth? Christianity says emphatically No.

## II

What, then, according to the Christian understanding of man, is wrong with these views? In view of what was said in the preceding chapter the answer will be clear. It is that none of these views does justice to the fact that man is primarily and distinctively a person in a world of personal relationships; and, in particular, none comes even within sight of the fact that absolutely basic and central in this personal world is the infinite and eternal personal reality, the source of all being, whom we call God. All these views are in varying ways atheistic; that is to say, they do not hold that there is anything in the nature of divine personal purpose, other than and above

[2] Italics mine.

humanity, with which men have to deal. As against this, Christianity affirms that man is first, last, and all the time a person; and that as such he stands first, last, and all the time in relation to the eternal Person, to God. Of course he stands in relation to finite persons as well, and, as we saw earlier, the relation to finite persons is inseparable from the relation to the eternal Person; but the latter, in the nature of the case, is the prior, the basic and fundamental relationship.

So then here at last is the Christian view of the essential secret of human nature, of the distinctive "humanity of the human." It is that he is a person standing all the time in personal relationship to God. It is that relationship which constitutes him—MAN. It is important from the Christian point of view to take this statement quite rigorously. That perhaps needs some effort of mind. It is so easy to think that a man can first be a man and then *afterward* enter into relationship with God, by becoming, for the first time, perhaps, consciously religious; or that he can cease to have relationship to God by ceasing to be consciously religious. We even speak of "godless" men. This, as I understand it, Christianity emphatically repudiates. It emphatically repudiates the idea that a man's relationship to God begins or ceases at the point where he begins or ceases to believe in God, or even to think about him. On the contrary, it says that man is distinctly man at all only because—whether he knows it or not, whether he likes it or not—he stands, right down to the innermost core and essence of his being, in the profoundest possible relationship to God all the time in an order of persons.

If, as is impossible, he could wrench himself out of that relationship, he would cease to be MAN. For when God creates a man, he creates that relationship by the same act—without the relationship there would be no man. Taken literally the phrase "a godless man" is a contradiction in terms.

What, then, is this relationship to God which is so deeply and foundationally constitutive of human life? In consonance with its whole personalist viewpoint Christianity says that, whatever else it may involve, there is at the very heart of it the element of claim—that is to say, a requirement which man is free to reject, but which he cannot escape. He can no more escape it than he can escape being a human person; but he can reject it, for if he could not reject it, equally he would not be a human person.

What, then, is the claim? The answer is: God claims man for complete obedience in complete trust, for complete trust in complete obedience. Yes, but what does this mean in terms of our actual, everyday existence as men? What, in practical life, is the content of the divine claim? Here what we said earlier about the other pole of the personal world comes in. The divine claim always draws its practical content from the claim of finite persons upon us. The two claims, the divine claim and the human claim, are not to be separated from one another. Man is called to obey and trust God by loving his brethren; and he cannot deeply and truly meet the claim of his brethren to his love save in complete obedience and trust toward God. In obedience and trust toward the eternal Person, in love toward finite persons—in these, inseparably bound together, and in these alone, does man realize his maturity as a person and become complete man.

We can now return to the question with which we began: What is it that, according to the Christian view, has gone so profoundly wrong with human life? The answer is that it is this quite basic relationship to God, lying at the root of man's whole distinctive nature as man, which has gone wrong. Men have rejected, and do reject, this claim of God upon them. It has been possible for it to go wrong precisely because it is a relationship of claim in a free personal world. It is only in the free personal world that you can have a relationship which can at one and the same time be deeply constitutive of a thing's nature and yet can also in any intelligible sense be said to go wrong; in the world of impersonal nature nothing, strictly speaking, can go wrong.

No doubt a tree which is stunted in growth or half eaten by parasites offends us; we feel something has gone wrong. But clearly something has gone wrong only in relation to our own desires and purposes. So far as impersonal nature is concerned nothing has gone wrong at all. Given the forces at work, the result is inevitable and quite in order. That this is so is shown by the fact that if our purposes require it, we are quite prepared to reverse the judgment and to think of a stunted tree as entirely right and satisfactory, as in a Japanese landscape; and as for parasites that devour, we ourselves are not a little devouring in relation to trees—or at any rate to their fruits. A wasp eating my greengages offends me; it is part of the problem of evil. But I do not mind stripping them myself; it is part of a harvest festival. A boa constrictor eating a deer shocks us. We vaguely think of the boa constrictor as evil and the deer as maltreated and offended against. But so far as impersonal nature is concerned everything is in order, and the boa constrictor is as innocent and blameless as the gentle deer. Nothing has gone wrong. It would be foolish to think of the deer as having a claim on the boa constrictor, which the latter wickedly rejects. It would be foolish to say to the boa constrictor, "Come now, pull yourself together; be a true boa constrictor." It is a true boa constrictor. Everything is in order.[3]

The descriptions and definitions of this fundamental wrongness in human life have been infinitely varied in the history of men's thought. All touch upon some important aspect of it precisely because it is such a foundational thing, affecting sooner or later every activity of man's life. Some have described it as disobedience and rebellion; others, as pride; others, as unbelief; others, as worldliness; others, as concupiscence or inordinate desire; others, as sensuality or carnal-mindedness or animality. Most common of all is the description of it as selfishness —self-will, self-seeking, anxiety for the self. But I venture to think that the understanding of it which goes deepest is the one we have been following.

By man's sin we mean a great refusal which man per-

---

[3] I recall that G. K. Chesterton has a similar thought to this somewhere. The view that the so-called "evil" in nature is itself an indirect result of the sin of man, or of some cosmic fall—so that it cannot strictly be spoken of as "in order"—is highly speculative, and I do not discuss it here. It does not affect the point I have been making.

sists in making at the center of his being, that centermost point where the claim of God—and, inseparably from that, the claim of his fellows—meets him and constitutes him a distinctively human person. In one way or another he rejects God's claim, and this means of necessity—since it is part of the very definition of a person that he acts under the form of self-awareness and self-direction—that he puts himself, puts the beloved ego, without a rival, on the throne. Those descriptions of man's wrongness which put the emphasis on selfishness or egotism are, therefore, nearest the truth. But in so far as they make no reference to the claim of God and to its constitutive relationship to the human person, they do not go to the heart of the matter, nor can they explain why the effects and consequences of sin should be of the tragic and far-reaching kind which we know them to be. On the Christian view sin, having to do with the ultimate core and basis of distinctively human personal life, *must* have such consequences. When the foundation slips and cracks, the whole house twists and splits and in the end may collapse altogether.

## III

The first, and perhaps most disabling, consequence is blindness. Man becomes increasingly unable to see the truth concerning himself, to discern the true meaning and uses of his life. He becomes increasingly unable to know what God's will for him, and claim upon him, are, and even to know that there is a personal God at all. There are at least two reasons for this blinding effect of sin.

First, it is obvious that if we see things from the wrong center, we must see them out of focus and perspective, distorted, and sometimes even completely upside down. If God and God's claim are—according to the essential constitution of things—the true center of the personal world, and I persist, in my freedom, in putting myself at the center, I must get everything wrong. It is like looking at a picture the wrong way up—the lines and colors seem in complete confusion, save perhaps for one or two accidental patterns and vague suggestions of identifiable objects which I think I can discern in it. Turn it the right way up, and at once I get an impression of the unity and harmony of the whole even though there is still some of its meaning which I can only partially discern.

This blinding effect of egocentricity is indeed a commonplace of everyday life, as well as of contemporary psychology. Its extreme expression is to be seen in the paranoiac, who twists everything, even the most innocent remarks and acts, into evidences of a sinister plot against his beloved ego. But in much less extreme forms it is familiar enough in us all. The Christian view sees in this egocentric blindness far more than an amiable weakness which only in extreme cases has disastrous consequences. It sees in it rather the evidence of a radical perversion of the whole life. We need to ask why egocentricity should be thus blinding. If the personal world were built on another pattern—the pattern, say, of the teaching of Nietzsche—egotism might well be the only clear glass through which the truth could be discerned. But it is in fact a clouding and distorting medium, and the reason is that the personal world is not built on Nietzschean lines. The center of it is not the ego; it is God.

The second reason why sin blinds has to do, once again, with the fact that God's claim upon man is written into the very constitution of his being—or, as we have already put it, though man can refuse it, he cannot escape it. He can no more escape it than he can escape being a man. The claim of God is upon him and in him all the time—because he is a man. What is the result? For the sake of his own peace of mind there begins in the sinner's mind a process of disguising from himself the real nature of his self-centered desires, his refusal of the claim of God and of his neighbor. He veils them in a fog of more or less clever sophistication and self-deception; he indulges, almost unconsciously, in what the psychologists have taught us to call rationalization; he uses his reason, which is part of his God-given status as a person, to persuade himself that the claims are other than they are, or that they do not apply to *him* at the moment. This also is a familiar enough process. We smile at such self-deception—in others!

Yet it is in fact no smiling matter. It is a symptom of something gravely wrong and dangerous. The grave danger is that it puts at the very heart of our being the need for, and the habit of, radical insincerity. Sin and insincerity always go together; and insincerity is, and must be, blinding. As I have said elsewhere,[4] it does not go deep enough to say that hypocrisy is the tribute sin pays to virtue; rather must we say that it is the

[4] *The World and God* (1935), p. 193.

tribute which man pays to his essential and inescapable humanity, to the inalterable constitution of his own being, built—as it is—upon the claim of God.

The second main consequence of man's refusal of the claim of God is that he tends in greater or less degree to lose his status and integrity as a person. Let me illustrate this by reference to those four types of view of human nature of which I spoke at the beginning of this chapter—or rather by those admitted facts of our human nature which, we said, give these views their plausibility. I shall suggest that in each case these facts begin to get out of hand, and become destructive of man's integrity and status as a person, precisely at the point where men fail to center their lives in the claim of God meeting them in the claim of their neighbor.

Thus, first, take what we called the naturalistic view, which regards man as entirely subject to all kinds of forces which mold and condition him to this or that kind of behavior. As I have said, there is truth in this. People certainly can be manipulated and conditioned —human nature *is* very plastic. This is not in itself a bad thing. The upbringing of children is largely a matter of molding them without their consent by all sorts of influences brought to bear upon them. But everything depends upon the ultimate purpose and aim of the molding—upon whether it looks forward to, and plans for, a time when the child shall stand free of such mere molding and conditioning, as an independent person, as one who walks by his own insight and loyalties and is *not* at the mercy of every influence that plays upon him.

Until a man can so stand free, he is not a person, as I said earlier.

What, then, is to set a man upright upon his feet—to establish him a person in spite of this valuable, yet always dangerous, plasticity of his nature, and the constant temptation it offers to others to misuse it? We reply: The only thing that can do this is the strong and abiding sense that every one of us, in all our dealings with one another, is, as a person, under the claim of God. Only such a strong sense will check in me the desire *merely* to manipulate people; only such a strong sense will make me resistant to those who are seeking thus merely to manipulate me. By the same argument, in proportion as this claim of God is not recognized and obeyed in human life, all human relationships become unresistant to deterministic forces and take a downward trend toward the impersonal. Thus—to take one contemporary example—propaganda. Propaganda, I suppose, is not necessarily bad. It is right to try to bring home to others the truth as we know it. Yet propaganda, in many of its forms, and most of all, perhaps, in its war forms, is one of the plainest evidences of human sin. But, observe, it is not merely those who unscrupulously use propaganda who manifest sin in their readiness merely to condition and manipulate their fellows. The people who are thus influenced by propaganda, who lack any power of resistance to it, also manifest sin. If to propagandize is an evidence of sin, to be propagandizable is so almost as much.

Then, second, take the cultural or high-brow view

of man. Once again, Christianity does not question the truth that is in this view. On the contrary, it sees in man's capacity for culture, for the creative seeking of ideal values in art and music and literature, an essential part of that distinctively personal life which God has bestowed upon him. I want only to point out the often horrible and perverting egotism which invades and takes possession of the cultural life, bringing with it a subtle impersonalism, as soon as it loses its true center in the claim of God meeting man in the claim of the neighbor —an impersonalism which is the more dangerous because it disguises itself as a disinterested seeking of the ideal values of truth and beauty.

Take, for example, the principle "art for art's sake." This principle was, I suppose, first promulgated in order to protect the pursuit of art from the distraction of other motives, and particularly from the corruption of commercialized self-seeking. As such it has a lofty sound and, in relation to certain historic periods and personal situations, a partial justification. But it does not, and cannot, succeed in its intention, because in fact nothing can really protect man from these things save a humble sense of the claim of God upon him meeting him always in the claim of his fellow.[5] Without that "art for art's sake"—as I once heard the late William Temple say— becomes art for nobody's sake; for to speak of "art" as such is to speak, after all, of an impersonal abstraction; and that means it becomes in due time art for the artist's sake, art for the sake of the artist's own self-expression,

[5] See, further, pp. 126, 138.

with no questions raised as to whether he has a self worth expressing or whether other selves have claims in the matter at all. Thus self creeps back into the center again. A corrupting picture, a bawdy book, is held to be justified if it can be claimed to be good art; its relation to the destiny of other persons is a matter of comparative indifference.[6] This is, I say, rank impersonalism, and it is inevitable so soon as man's life, even in its highest creative reaches, loses its true center in the claim of God. The only right principle from the Christian point of view is art for God's sake and for man's, neither to be separated from the other.

Take now the vitalist view of man, the insistence on the instinctive, passional, side of man, on the fact that he is body as well as spirit, instinct as well as reason, organic flesh and blood as well as soul. This also enshrines a side of the truth which Christianity has no interest in denying. But does not the very necessity which some have felt to insist on this side of man against views which do not do justice to it bear witness to a fundamental split— a fundamental lack of integrity or wholeness in the human person—of which, I suppose, we are all aware in ourselves? There *is* a conflict in all of us between reason and instinct, flesh and spirit, conscience and desire, however it may be described. So deep-seated and persistent is the conflict that it has been widely held to be the root cause of all that has gone wrong in human life. The cause of all the trouble, it is said, is that man is es-

[6] It might be questioned whether a corrupting picture or a bawdy book ever could be a great work of art, but we need not go into that.

sentially soul or spirit incongruously attached to or immersed in, a physical and animal body; and in the at-
tempts which men have made to deal with the trouble
there has been a pendulum swing between an asceticism
which goes too far in its denial of the claims of the bodily
and instinctive life and an antiasceticism which has gone
too far in the assertion of them.

Plainly neither is a real solution, for the split in the
total human person remains, And just here the distinctive and deep Christian insight comes in, for Christianity
does not say that this conflict is the cause of the "having
gone wrong–ness" of human life, but rather, on the contrary, it is the "having gone wrong–ness" which causes
the conflict, at any rate in the disabling and destructive
form in which we know it and have to deal with it. Once
again it is the wrong relation to God, which we call sin,
which has split and disintegrated the human person.
Man is not—as the Greeks and some false forms of
Christian doctrine, unduly influenced by the Greeks,
have taught—spirit temporarily imprisoned in flesh, soul
miserably tethered to a body, but a single, unitary, body-
spirit person made wholly for God, and therefore finding
his wholeness only in God. It is because that fundamental
central relationship to God has broken down that the
unity of spirit and body has also broken down. It is like
the withdrawal of some central pivot which holds the
parts of some complex piece of machinery in a co-opera-
tive harmony. Break it, or twist it, or take it out, and at
once the parts lose their harmony, grinding against

one another, liable to break loose and damage anyone who gets in their way.

Or, finally, take what we called the collectivist or group view of man. Once again, this view confronts us with plain facts about human nature which Christianity has no concern to question. God has created us as members of groups, communities, nations, and nothing can alter it. Yet, plainly enough, this side of human existence is today in the direst conflict and confusion, running out into the grossest impersonalism in men's dealing with one another, and into horrible discords and tensions within the personal lives of individual men and women.

It is hardly necessary to illustrate this, but consider what is in some ways the supreme problem in this sphere today—the problem of instituting an increasing control and direction of national life from the center and at the same time leaving room for that freedom and initiative of the individual which are the very breath of personal life; the problem of how to plan social life thoroughly and effectively without that enslaving of the individual to the group which is totalitarianism, but equally without individual freedom's involving a return to the anarchic and predatory competition of the last century, which in many of its effects was as depersonalizing and degrading as totalitarianism itself has proved to be. Or consider how the disorder of our national and international life is reflected in disorder within the personal lives of individual men and women. Men find themselves inwardly torn to pieces by conflicts of apparent loyalties and duties, by choices not between good and evil but between greater and lesser evils. This reaches a horrible climax in modern war, where for the sake of persons men must maim and destroy persons in as wholesale and impersonal way as they would destroy locusts or rats—until for the sake of inward peace they must persuade themselves that there is no real difference after all, and that their enemies, when all is said, are only locusts or rats in human form.

What, then, is the source of this confusion and impersonalism and disintegration? Christianity says that it is sin, it is the fact that human life has lost its true center in the claim of God meeting us all equally in all men equally. Christianity does not indeed say anything so silly as that if only men would rightly believe in God every problem would vanish overnight. It does not even say that so long as men do *not* believe in God nothing whatever can be done to improve social and international arrangements, or to restrict and restrain within limits the worst consequences of the all-devouring egotisms of men and peoples. But it does say, and I think experience supports what it says, that so long as this basic wrongness in human life is not set right—the wrongness, that is to say, of its relationship to God— these problems can be solved only superficially and temporarily, for every so-called "solution" will contain within it the seeds of its own collapse.

Our discussion of this last point has brought us to the third main thing of which we must take note in considering the consequences which flow, and must flow, from sin.

Just because the personal order is that close-knit

continuum of relationships between a man, his neighbor, and God which we have tried to set forth, it follows that the effects and consequences of any one individual's sin cannot possibly be confined to himself. That seems self-evident. Yet that the innocent suffer by and for the deeds of the guilty is frequently spoken of as though it were a specially dark and perplexing problem. It is indeed a very solemn and dread fact, and as such it is part of the solemn and dread fact of sin; but that it is dark and mysterious in any special or additional way I have never been able to see. The supposition that it is rests, once again, upon an inadequate understanding of the personal order in which God has placed us. It rests on a falsely individualistic and atomistic view of personality, as though it might conceivably be possible, if only things were arranged differently, for a human person to live to himself like a cat and still remain a human person.

But if our understanding of these matters is correct, that is impossible. The bringing into existence of human persons necessarily involves that they suffer by, and for, one another's wrong attitudes and deeds. The one is not possible without the other. Sin being a perversion of personal relations, the consequences of it are bound to permeate into the lives of all, whatever may be the degree of their individual contributions to the whole sorry state of affairs. No man can be judged wholly responsible for the darkness and perversity and discord of his own being, for he could be *wholly* responsible for it only by being an isolated person, that is, by ceasing to be a person at all. On the other hand, no man can be judged wholly *without* responsibility for it, for in that case also he would not be a person. In some deep way we are corrupted by the general sinful state of humanity into which we are born, and yet we make the corruption our own, and make it still more deeply part of us, by our own choice and decision, by putting our own causality as persons into it. We are not wholly responsible, and yet we are not wholly without responsibility.

It is along this line of thought that we can discern the meaning, and the deep and abiding truth, of the so-called doctrines of "original sin" and "total depravity." I observe that many of our contemporaries, both inside and outside the Church—especially perhaps in the United States—still react against these doctrines with a violence which is hardly compatible with clear discernment of truth. That much dubious theology has been attached to them in the past is not to be denied, but it is extremely superficial to reject them out of hand for that reason. The phrases themselves may well be discarded because of their dubious associations and misleading overtones of meaning, but let not the dread facts of the human situation to which they refer be slurred over.

The truth of the doctrine of "original sin" is precisely what we have just been saying, namely, that the whole close-knit, human, personal order into which we are born, into which we must be born if we are to come into existence as persons at all, is in fact, and in another sense, no longer an order; it is a disorder, and its disorder instantly becomes part and parcel of our personal existence, even before we become conscious of ourselves as persons and can be deemed in any way responsible for it—though, as I have said, in due course we also put our own personal responsibility into it. Sin thus meets and conditions us at the very point of our origin. It is *origin*-al sin. A newborn child, for all its lovely freshness and innocence, thus constitutes a problem for God, even though there is no call to describe it in Calvin's words as "odious and abominable" to God.

As for the doctrine of "total depravity," it does not, or should not, mean—as has been often pointed out—that everything in human life is foul and beastly and depraved; everything in human life is plainly not foul and beastly and depraved. But it does mean that everything in human life is affected by the fundamental wrong relationship to God which lies at the very root of man's being. The totality of man's being is affected. But that is not to say that everything in his being is so totally affected that there is no gleam of light and goodness anywhere at all. The doctrine of total depravity, I repeat, is not that everything in man's being is utterly foul; it is rather that even the good things can become utterly foul, and even when they are far from warranting so strong a term as that, nevertheless they are always infected with sin and fall short—far short—of the best, and of what God intended them to be when he created man.

# Chapter IV

# GOD'S ACTION IN CHRIST

CHRISTIANITY has a distinctive view of what has gone wrong with human life; it also has a distinctive view of the way in which what has gone wrong can be set right. In the preceding chapter we have spoken of the former. We now come to the latter, and in so doing we come to the innermost heart and center of what the Christian faith has to say about God and men and their relations with one another.

There is one conviction which is common to all Christian communities, giving them, in spite of their many and often deep differences, a fundamental unity with one another; a conviction which is, further, peculiar to all Christian communities, giving their belief and conduct such distinctive quality as they may possess; one which, finally, is acknowledged by all Christian communities as being, however variously interpreted and expounded in detail, the very core and essence of their witness to mankind. That conviction is that in order to set right the profound "having gone wrong–ness" of human life the infinite Person, God, has himself taken action. He has made a new and unparalleled entry into the midst of the finite personal world, into the midst of history, an entry the purpose of which is to save and restore. This action, this entry, is the coming of Jesus Christ into the world. Here surely

is the minimal content and definition of Christian orthodoxy—Jesus Christ is God savingly in action, once and
for all, "for us men and our salvation." Therefore he is in
the fullest sense unique, final, adequate, indispensable, for
the setting right of human life. In the apostle Paul's
words, "God was in Christ reconciling the world to himself."

It is important to say, particularly in view of some of
the things we shall come to later, that according to the
Christian faith this divine saving action in Christ is
not yet a fully completed action. It is still going on.
The advent of Jesus Christ marks a new beginning—
God's new beginning. God at that point in history
took hold of the gone-wrong personal world of
men in a new and, to repeat the phrase, once-and-for-
all way. But he has still, so to say, got hold of it; his grip
has not loosened; he is still at work with the wrongness
—in and through Christ—and the completion of the
work is still to come. Indeed, as we shall see, it is part of
the Christian faith that the completion of God's saving
work in Christ—the full realization of his kingdom—is
to be thought of as transcending history, transcending
this world of space and time altogether.

It is this conviction concerning God's final and adequate action in Christ which from the beginning put the
distinctively Christian word "gospel" so inevitably on the
lips of those who sought to bring the Christian message
to mankind. For the same reason the primary documents
about Christ are called gospels, and not lives or biographies, though they are lives or biographies of a kind.

Christianity was never, and is not now, primarily a philosophy, an attempt to formulate a world view which shall comprehend so far as possible in one perspective everything of which we have knowledge and experience. No doubt the Christian message can be made the basis of a world view—it would have to be a deeply personalistic world view and would have sharply to reject some other world views—but it is not primarily such a world view. Again, Christianity was not and is not primarily a system of doctrines, such as learned theologians excogitate, though it implies and leads on to such a system, and such a system will have its place in Christian thought and experience. Nor certainly was it, or is it, just a matter of giving people moral advice and exhortation, holding up to them the example of a superlatively fine life and telling them to try very hard to be like that. The teaching and the example of Jesus Christ are important, and have always been felt to be so by Christian believers, but they are not the primary message. The primary message was, and is, that something has happened, and is happening, in the world of persons. What has happened, and is happening, is a new and unprecedented divine action. God has gone into action, is in action, for us men and our salvation—in Jesus Christ. Wherefore the Christian message is primarily announcement, good news, gospel.

In turning to this quite central and distinctive Christian affirmation we are obviously turning to a subject whose far-reaching and profound implications have engaged the reflection of some of the greatest minds all down the centuries. We certainly cannot do more here than touch upon one or two of the outermost fringes of it; we must select without so much as even hinting at many deep and important and puzzling matters. And the principle of selection must obviously be what we have taken as our main guiding interest—namely, the relevance of the Christian message to the world of persons, and the task which is laid upon us to make that relevance as plain and persuasive as we can to any of our contemporaries who are prepared to listen.

In pursuing that task it is important to insist that this grand, central affirmation of God's saving action in Christ shall not be approached in a merely prejudiced way. It is very easy for us modern folk to bring with us attitudes of mind which, in so far as we are conscious of them—very often we are not aware of them at all— seem to us to be utterly reasonable, but which on examination prove to be scarcely more than prejudice and presupposition. It is very easy to regard passing fashions as final categories of thought or principles of judgment. I have not infrequently met people whose primary reaction to the Christian assertion of God's action in Christ is quite evidently, "Impossible! Unbelievable!" even though they may be too polite to use such blunt terms.

But why impossible? Why unbelievable? The question is usually not asked. We have surely the right, and the duty, to protest against such a shutting of the mind, such a decision in advance as to what can or cannot happen in this infinitely mysterious universe in which we find ourselves alive. No doubt, as was said in an earlier chapter, we have to be on our guard against an undisciplined and uncritical credulity; but equally we have to be on our guard against an undisciplined and unreflective incredulity.

It will be worth while, I think, to consider two of the prejudices which lie behind the initial incredibility which is felt, in some quarters, to attach to the Christian affirmation concerning God's unique saving action in Christ. They both have to do with what we have already spoken of so much, namely, the failure to give proper place to, and to grasp the distinctive nature of, the personal world.

## I

The first is a prejudice which is to be found even in those who are prepared to give some sort of place in their outlook upon life to religious feeling, who are even willing to use the term "God." It is a prejudice against the idea that God can ever be properly thought of as *breaking into* human history, as acting *ad hoc* and relevantly to a human situation of need.

There are, I think, two causes of this prejudice, intimately bound up with one another. One is the curious tendency of the human mind, whenever it combines some capacity for philosophic reflection with some capacity for religious feeling, to betake itself to a vague sort of pantheism. Pantheism is a slippery term, with many different meanings and shades of meaning; but speaking generally we may say that it means the view that all individual things and events whatsoever—

100

*all,* including human persons and their needs, including also those things which we generally judge to be evil— are parts, or aspects, or manifestations or vehicles of a close-knit, all-embracing unity—a unity which, if we could grasp it in its wholeness, we should see to be wholly harmonious and satisfying and good. This all-embracing unity, which is already "there" in its perfect completeness, is what we mean, or should mean, by the term "God." And religion, is, or should be, just man's endeavor to lay hold of this unity, and be laid hold of by it—in what one modern writer of this school calls "moments of transcendence"—so that by so doing he may find rest and peace. Religion is a matter of cosmic feeling or, as it has been put, "you mix yourself up with the landscape and call it religion."

It is clear that according to this usage God cannot ever be said to act specially and purposefully and relevantly to particular historical situations; for the whole universe is God in action, and he is equally in action in every part of it, if indeed, on this basis you can properly predicate action of him at all. Still less can you speak of him as acting relevantly to *what has gone wrong;* for, on this view, nothing has gone wrong, or could go wrong. As a whole, and also in respect of all its parts, the universe, according to this interpretation, is already a perfectly realized harmony and completely satisfactory; that, indeed, is why it is felt to be legitimate to call it "God." It is clear also that from this standpoint there is nothing at all urgent or challenging in the thought of God; for God as the realized harmony and perfection of universal being is just "there" all the time, whatever we think or do about it. Indeed, our thinking and doing are already part of the perfect unity of the whole, and, therefore, in the last analysis, there is nothing to choose between one sort of thinking and doing and another—between, say, the religious man, taking on a soulful look when in a "moment of transcendence" he contemplates the aesthetic unity of the all, and the film star who confessed that he found the best way to induce a soulful look was to contemplate in imagination a juicy and succulent steak. Pantheism is in fact a very comfortable religion, and it is the more attractive to some because it has the appearance of being highly intellectual and philosophical; it is much more comfortable to profess a pantheistic philosophy than to believe in the personal God who acts and seeks us and *claims* us. The pantheist's God makes no claims; he simply allows himself to be looked at, as Brunner says [1]—if, that is, you happen to like looking at him.

The other cause of this prejudice against the idea of God's taking action is once again the tyranny exercised over so many modern minds by laboratory science, and in particular by the notion that such science requires us to think of the universe as being in all its aspects just a vast system of cause-effect relationships in which all events are bound together by rigidly necessary and unbreakable laws. I suspect that one reason why so many modern people, when they are minded to be religious, betake themselves to pantheism is that they

[1] *Man in Revolt* (Eng. tr., 1939), p. 432.

vaguely feel that a pantheistic view of the world harmonizes better with this supposedly all-inclusive and overriding scientific requirement. It is alleged, or at least vaguely felt, that to admit the possibility of God's deliberately acting into human affairs—whether in the coming of Christ or in other ways—to admit the possibility that God by an act of will might bring about events which apart from that act of will would not take place, is to admit the possibility of interference with, or suspension of, the so-called laws of nature; and this, so it is supposed, would make scientific work impossible.

It is manifestly not possible in a study such as this to engage in a refutation of this somewhat naïve view.[2] I have already pointed out [3] that it ignores the distinctively personal world in which we all, scientist included live, and move, and have our being. Furthermore it takes no account of the problem of knowledge, of the fact that there is not only a known world but also a mind knowing it. It is in fact a colossal oversimplification. Unfortunately, as with all oversimplifications, the reasons against it go deeper and are more difficult to state and to understand than the reasons in favor of it. This constitutes a real difficulty in the way of getting through the prejudices of the contemporary mind. But at least we are entitled to point out—if we do no more—how many great and deep minds have wrestled with precisely this problem of how to conceive a world which at one and

---

[2] I have tried to deal with it elsewhere, in *The World and God* (1935), pp. 145-79, and *Towards Belief in God* (1942), pp. 213-30.

[3] See above, pp. 41-47.

the same time contains persons free to initiate action and yet also is thoroughly amenable to scientific research and control by those persons. The felt necessity to wrestle with the problem at least shows that a too-easy dismissal of the question must rest far more on prejudice and impressionism than on sound knowledge and thought.

## II

The second reason why some find an initial incredibility in the Christian assertion of God's saving action in Christ is that their minds are possessed with the belief that there is an inherent and necessary law of progress governing human affairs. This, as has often enough been pointed out, is a distinctively modern belief, being indeed a secularized version of the Christian doctrine of providence from which historically it would appear to be derived; and though it has received some nasty jolts during the last two or three decades, it still dominates a great many people's minds far more than they realize.[4]

It is not difficult to see how such a belief as this prejudices the mind unconsciously against the Christian gospel of the divine saving action into history in Christ.

In the first place, if human affairs are progressing by some inherent necessity, any kind of extra *ad hoc* saving action on the part of God becomes quite superfluous.

[4] Especially in the United States, though even in battered and disillusioned Europe the belief in a necessary ascent of the historical process toward better things, through conflict and collapse, is a central article in the communist creed. A creed published in the United States begins with the article, "I believe in myself," and proceeds to assert, among other things, that "onward, ever onward, presses the creative life. Higher, clearer than ever before, it speaks in the faith of the modern man."

No doubt a doctrine of necessary evolution and progress can—as in communist belief—make room for incidental evils and discords, such as we know have occurred, and do occur, in human affairs; but any sort of radical bedevilment or "having gone wrong–ness" in the historical process, calling for any radical new beginning or new action, is clearly inadmissible. One can admit the reefs and the breakers, the back eddies and the swirls, of a rocky coast without in the least entertaining the idea that, unless someone takes action and blows them up, there will not be a high tide.

Then, in the second place, on the basis of this belief in an always ongoing and inevitable progress people, I observe, often react against the idea that there should appear in the midst of history anything in the nature of a finality such as Christianity asserts God's active and saving self-disclosure in Christ to be. Such an assertion, it is said, puts a premature barrier to, and limitation upon, that continuous moving forward into fresh knowledge and experience which characterizes all our human life and, indeed, gives it its excitement and zest; it binds us to an ever-receding past; there can be no such finality at any one point in the constant and inevitable ascent. "Onward, ever onward, presses the creative life." Anybody who claimed to have been given a finality of knowledge in, say, biology would be laughed to scorn; how absurd then to suppose that in Jesus Christ there has come into man's life any sort of final disclosure of God. Let us take up each of these two points in turn.

First, consider the conviction that there is an inherent

inevitability in human progress, requiring nothing but its own impetus to carry us to ever higher reaches of human achievement and well-being. Such a conviction obviously far outstrips—and must in the nature of the case far outstrip—the empirical evidence. No evidence available to the human mind could possibly enable us to predict with such assurance the ultimate outcome of the infinitely complex factors which determine the unfolding of the human story even on this planet alone; indeed, the available evidence could as well be used, as it has in fact not seldom been used, to support a thoroughly pessimistic view of the future. As has already been said, there is certainly not lacking today much to suggest that something has gone radically wrong with mankind. In other words, belief in inevitable progress is really an expression of faith. It is none the worse for that, for without some sort of faith in the future men cannot carry on. Christianity itself has faith in the future of humanity, because it believes in the sovereign and active and saving wisdom and love of God. But the point is, seeing this modern belief in inevitable progress *is* faith, and not, as it is sometimes represented to be, an empirically based and intellectually emancipated viewpoint, it would surely be far better to have it out in the open and examine it *as a faith,* and to compare it thoughtfully *as a faith* with the Christian faith, rather than to allow it merely to prejudice the mind from the outset against the latter.

If we do that, the Christian faith in the future of our race proves itself to be far deeper, more realistic, and more adequate. Many reasons might be given for this judgment, but I content myself with developing one reason only—one which is in line with our thought throughout this study. This reason is, that the Christian faith does justice, as the other view does not, to the world of persons. I make two points in support of this statement.

First, the notion of an inherently necessary progress moving on irresistibly to its predestined end, if it is strictly adhered to, and not helped out by unconscious borrowing from theistic faith, degrades man from his status as a morally responsible person whose choices and decisions really do make significant difference to the unfolding of events, whether for good or for ill. Taken strictly, it reduces the whole thing to a stage play in which the actors appear to shape the course of events but in reality only repeat lines already written, in a sequence already laid down. Yet, as William James says, if there is one thing which is certain, it is that history does not feel like a stage play, nor can it be lived as though it were a stage play. Why not? Because it is really a free personal world.

The truth of what James says is illustrated by the inconsistent way in which the orthodox communist proclaims his conviction; for he will assert the necessary dialectic movement of history as it moves through the dictatorship of the proletariat to its predestined end in the classless state, and then in the same breath denounce with the utmost indignation the exceeding great wickedness of the capitalist and bourgeois classes. Yet if the movement forward really is necessarily predetermined, and at the same time necessarily "dialectic"—that is, by tension and conflict—then surely the wretched capitalist appears within it only as an indispensable and valuable item in the process, and no more ought to be blamed than the actor ought to be tried for murder when he comes off the stage from playing Macbeth. But, it may be said, what basis of confidence in the future have we if we do take the freedom of morally responsible persons seriously? Does not that involve the possibility that man's evil choices, man's sin, may send everything permanently and irretrievably to ruin? To this we must answer that there is no basis of confidence, there is no escaping that grim possibility, if human beings in all their limitation and "having gone wrong–ness" are the *only persons* who are actively concerned in the historical process.

But then it is precisely this that Christianity, in its massive adequacy and consistency, denies. For it asserts that there is at work in history, not a mechanical and impersonal necessity which, I repeat, degrades the personal status of man, but the infinitely profound wisdom and patience of God, the infinite Person, who knows, in that same infinite wisdom and patience, how both to respect the personal status of the men and women he has made and yet to keep hold of the whole process and to bring it under his rule. And in particular he has acted, and is acting, in the midst of the "having gone wrong–ness" of the personal world, in Jesus Christ. No doubt there is in this thought of the divine action and control in history much that baffles, and must baffle, our understanding; but all faith as to the future—I repeat, we cannot live without some faith—must go beyond understanding at some point. Nevertheless, it may well be argued that on the whole the Christian thought of an infinite personal wisdom which may be trusted to keep its head amid the infinitely complex contingencies of human history is less baffling to the mind than the thought of an inherent necessity—which is credited with doing the same thing, although *ex hypothesi* it has no head to keep.[5]

The second point I make in support of my statement that the Christian faith does more justice to the world of persons is this: If you limit your hopes for the future of humanity, as so many modern believers in inevitable progress do, to the realization of a perfect state of society in this earth and this earth alone, then you reduce every person who lives prior to the coming of that perfect society to the status of a mere item in, or vehicle of, the process, with no intrinsic significance or worth in himself as a person at all. Once again, he suffers degradation as a person. For when the end state of perfection is reached, he will have vanished forever from the scene and have no part or lot in it—like an ant who, having produced a few eggs and gathered a bit of sugar for the ant heap and so contributed to the ant heap which is to be, is then perhaps crushed under the gardener's boot. What does it matter? She was probably a poor specimen of an ant anyway, with capitalist or bourgeois leanings! Thus, with perfect logical consistency, some of our con-

[5] In this sentence I have paraphrased and applied some words of Tennant in *Philosophical Theology*, Vol. II (1930), p. 108. See also my *Towards Belief in God* (1942), p. 202.

temporary believers in an impersonal, dialectic progress think nothing of liquidating a few thousand people. What does it matter? There are plenty more, and the process goes on.[6]

This impersonalism Christianity also escapes by its faith as to the future. How? By firmly insisting that the kingdom which God in the infinite wisdom and patience of his love will bring out of the awful travail and suffering of human history transcends the limits of this world altogether. By firmly insisting, too, that in relation to that kingdom all persons have an indefeasible significance, which nothing can take from them, not even the fact that they die and vanish from the earth. It is most important to realize this. The Christian belief that the divine saving action in Christ is completed, not in history, but beyond it, is once again part of its radical personalism; it is not a merely otherworldly fantasy.

It is along this same line of the intense and consistent personalism of the Christian interpretation of God's purpose in history that we answer the other objection urged by some moderns, namely, that the position ascribed by Christianity to Jesus Christ as the revelation of God puts a finality into the midst of human life, whereas in all other spheres our knowledge and understanding are moving forward all the time. This objection really involves a quite illegitimate identification of the way of knowledge in the sphere of persons with the way of knowledge in such impersonal spheres as chemistry or

[6] For an impressive, indeed terrible, *exposé* of the fanatical logical consistency of this attitude, see A. Koestler, *Darkness at Noon*.

biology or any other field of scientific inquiry. If it is true that the necessary result of wrongness in the personal relations a man has with God and his fellows is an ever-increasing blindness to the truth concerning this whole central sphere of his life, then obviously there can be no progress in that sphere until the wrong–ness is set right and the blindness healed. The Christian belief is that God is in action in Jesus Christ in the midst of human life precisely in order to set right this wrongness and to heal this blindness. Clearly, if that belief is true at all, then the objection that it puts a premature limit on knowledge does not hold. Indeed, the exact opposite is the case. God's action in Christ takes the limits off; it opens the avenues of knowledge in the personal world; it certainly does not close them. The finality of Christ is his finality as reconciler in the personal world of God and man; it is his finality as healer of blindness; it is his finality, therefore, as *source* of light and truth—not as closure upon them.

## III

So much, then, for some of the prejudices which are apt to predispose the mind against the Christian affirmation concerning God's action in Christ. Can we now give some positive reasons through which we might invite a serious hearer to give it earnest consideration? As soon as we ask that question, a multitude of possible lines of thought suggest themselves. I propose to confine myself to one only—one which again is in harmony with the general course of our thought. If I have succeeded in carrying an interested reader thus far with me, I may then go on to ask him to take note of the profound consistency of the account the Christian message gives of the divine saving action with that whole personal realm which it insists on setting at the heart of its interpretation of God and man. The whole thing hangs together. After all, a deep and penetrating consistency—a consistency which reveals itself the more you dig into it and seek to illumine and interpret life by it—is always a good reason for giving any view serious consideration. Such a consistency is at least the beginning of that shining in its own light without which no truth can come home to us.

Let us ask: What, according to the Christian view, was it necessary for God's action in Christ to effect if it was to be really saving? The answer, in the light of all that has been said earlier, is: It had to effect at least three things.

First, it had to make plain to men, in face of the "having gone wrong–ness" of the personal world and in particular the blindness caused by it, the real nature of the personal world; and especially it had to make plain what we called in an earlier chapter the bipolarity of it—that is to say, the fact that a man stands always and inescapably in a critical relationship of claim and responsibility to God and to his fellows at one and the same time. The saving act had to be a disclosure and reaffirmation of the God-human structure of the personal world.

Second, it had to make plain to men, in face of men's blindness, what are right relations within the world of persons; that is to say, it had to make plain to them the claim of God for obedience and trust meeting them in the claim of their fellows for their love.

Third—and this is particularly important for understanding the method of the divine action in Christ—all this had to be made plain, and reaffirmed, in a way calculated to break through the darkness and resistance of men's egocentric, sinful minds the truth had to be thrust home, yet never in such a way as to coerce or override or manipulate men's minds; for if it did that, it would be false to the true nature of the personal world and, so far from unveiling it, would obscure it more deeply than ever. It had to be effective, yet not overriding.

It is, to say the least, difficult to see how all these things could be done otherwise than through confronting men with the truth in a historic personal life, itself embodying and participating in that personal order with which the salvation of man is centrally concerned. To take the points in the reverse order:

First, it is difficult to see how a disclosure of the truth concerning the human-divine personal world could be effective other than by taking the form of an utterly perfect and true concrete embodiment of human personal life, lived in the midst of, and confronting us out of the midst of, those very events and relationships which constitute our historical existence as persons. For it had to deal with the *actual* corruption and darkness which sin causes and must cause, and yet also it had to remain true to the personal world by not being merely coercively overriding but rather by evoking in men an inward response and consent. And in particular it was most necessary that it should thus confront us out of the midst of, and in relation to, human personal life as corrupted and darkened and embittered by sin, for it is in it as corrupted and darkened and embittered by sin that we have to live the new life which God through Christ is seeking to give us.

If anybody can suggest any other method which would fulfill the double condition laid down, it would be interesting to hear it; any other method would be, so far as I can see, either ineffective or not personal. Certainly the mere announcement of general truths concerning, say, the love and saving purpose of God, however frequently or eloquently uttered, could not be effective. To suppose that they could shows a very poor grasp either of the nature of personality or of the effects of sin. General truths cannot get right inside us, so to speak, and continue to get right inside us—challenging the will, stirring the feelings, breaking up our obstinate resistance. They cannot pierce the hard crust of our egotism—wtih its fears and prides and hates—and, when the crust reforms, pierce it again and again, letting in light, and again letting in light, bringing us to a true and deep penitence, making real and credible a divine pardon which no guilt can turn aside, and releasing, quickening, and cleansing our perverted and frustrated impulses toward our true personal life with God and with one another. Only truth in personal embodiment and action, truth meeting us and challenging us in the actual historical sinful situations which are the real stuff of our personal existence, could do all this.

Second, all this becomes even more evident when we consider the true nature of the personal world which the saving action of God had thus effectively, yet never impersonally, to bring home to the alienated and darkened minds of men. The most compendious description of that order which Christianity gives is that it is, or is meant to be, an order of love. What exactly it means to say that God's will—so far as it is concerned with persons—is love, and that the claim is made upon us to obey and trust that will in love to one another, we shall consider later in the light of the historic revelation in Christ.[7] This will be a necessary undertaking because it is part of the egocentric darkness in which we live that love so frequently becomes a weak and sloppy word on our lips.

We know, however, enough of what love is as a personal relationship to be able to see that the reality of love, and the all-commanding claim upon us which it carries, can be compellingly known only through its *active* self-manifestation and self-giving in the actual crises of men's personal history; in the logic of personal relationship only the deed can disclose and demonstrate the reality of love. And this is the more evidently so when for one reason or another there is a relationship of estrangement and distrust between persons. Then, indeed, general statements about love, however beautiful, and protestations of love, however eloquent, are of them-

[7] See below, Chap. VI.

selves impotent to penetrate the darkness. Indeed they make matters worse; for so immediately cognizant is the human mind of the logic of historic action that, so long as the deed is lacking, it is suspicious at once of an underlying unreality and insincerity, which is still further destructive of trust. And of course the final proof of love, beyond which it is not possible to go, is given when the deed involves that final and total giving of the self to the other: "Greater love hath no man than this, that a man lay down his life for his friends."

All this is self-evident, as self-evident in the personal sphere as the logic of propositions is self-evident in the sphere of mathematics; but the implications of it are not always seen. There is to be discerned through it what may be called the "necessity of history" in God's purpose—the necessity, that is to say, of a sphere of persons in relationship in which events take place through free and concrete decisions and *deeds*. There is also to be discerned part, at least, of the meaning of death in relation to the finite personal world and God's ordering of it, namely, that it affords opportunity for the last clinching proof in historical deed of that utter yielding of the whole being to the claim of God and the claim of the neighobor which is perfect love. And again there is to be discerned in all this, and this is our particular interest at the moment, the profound consistency of the Christian faith when it affirms that God's saving revelation of truth, of the real order of our life as persons, was made not through the imparting of general truths but through the historical personal life of Jesus Christ and supremely through his utter giving of himself to God and to man in the death on the cross. The rooting of the Christian faith in history, in a historical life and death, is part and parcel, once again, of its deep-going and radical personalism.

Third, and finally, there is the most fundamental point of all, namely, the essential bipolarity of the personal world whereby men are always in a relationship of claim to God and to one another at the same time. The two claims, we have insisted, are not to be separated from one another. Yet men in their sinfulness do continually tear them apart. Sometimes, indeed, men reject both the claim of God and the claim of the neighbor, neither fearing God nor regarding man; but more frequently, and perhaps more dangerously, they suppose that it is possible to meet the claims of God—or what they take to be such—while ignoring the claims of the neighbor; or—most common of all in these days of confessed or unconfessed humanism—they imagine that it is possible to meet the claims of the neighbor while ignoring the claims of God.

According to Christianity there is no possibility of any restoration of our life until these are inseparably fused and reintegrated with one another, so that whenever we look into a human face, we always see the claims of God, and whenever we look into the face of God, we always see the claims of man. Plainly, if that is what God has effectively to bring home to our sinful and egocentric hearts, it is no light task; and I for one find it hard to think how it could be done effectively, and yet not impersonally, save in the way that the Christian faith affirms it has been done and is being done, namely, by the appearance in history of a *person*—a person, I repeat, in whom there confronts us at one and the same time, in unclouded splendor and purity, the divine will of love itself and the concrete individuality of a man living the life of a man among men.

I am inclined to think that when we look at God's saving action in Christ from this angle, we reach what is perhaps the deepest religious understanding, as distinct from an attempt to think through its theoretical implications, of the central Christian affirmation of the appearance of the God-man in history—the Incarnation as we usually call it. The doctrine of the Incarnation is part of the radical personalism of Christianity and of its understanding of the true nature of the personal order. Christ is God revealing to our sinful blindness the two essential poles—divine and human—of our finite personal life. The "bipolarity" of Christ, if I may so put it, focuses and expresses that essential bipolarity of the personal world to which sin blinds our eyes. That certainly is how it has worked out in the lives of Christian men and women, who have been brought into an entirely new understanding of, and relation to, the personal world through Christ. When they have looked up into the face of God, they have seen always the human Christ, in some sense the representative and symbol of every member of that human race which he loved and for which he gave his life; when they have looked into the face of a man, they have seen the divine Christ, the love of God himself, claiming their love for that man.

118

# Chapter V

# THE HOLINESS OF GOD

THE Christian church has been in existence for nearly twenty centuries; that is to say, for nearly twenty centuries there have been countless men and women who, with all their divergent gifts, temperaments, cultures, traditions, historical situations, and tasks—in short, all their distinctive individuality as persons—have sought to live in the God-human personal world in the light of what they have believed to be God's own great saving act of revelation in Jesus Christ. That being so, one would expect two things to happen, which have in fact happened. First, one would expect that there would be built up in course of time a distinctive and identifiable group of common convictions concerning the personal world, concerning God and men and their relations with one another. Second, one would expect, precisely because it is a personal world which is being lived in, and dealt with, all the time, that into the building up of this common body of Christian beliefs there would always enter a considerable variety of detailed emphasis and interpretation; for personality and individuality and variety go together. As one passes into the realm of things, the less of individual variety there is, and the more easy it is in consequence to build up a detailed uniformity of belief concerning them.

This fact is not unimportant. People are always falling into two errors in this connection. One error is that they persistently underestimate the solid unanimity that there is in Christian thought and experience in respect of those central matters without which there would not be a distinctive Christian faith and way of life at all. They speak as though Christians were completely at sixes and sevens in belief, so that it is impossible for anyone to know what exactly the message is with which Christianity challenges the world. I do not wish to ignore this difficulty or to treat it as of no consequence, but it is often, I fear, turned into a mere excuse for escaping the challenge; in any case it is a gross and ignorant exaggeration. At the Edinburgh Conference held in 1937, at which there were present representatives of all the Christian churches with the one exception of the Roman Church, there was disclosed what one competent observer estimated to be a 90-per-cent agreement in respect of the broad, central doctrines of the Christian faith. The second error people make is that they persistently overestimate the significance of the very real differences in detailed belief and interpretation that there admittedly are. They speak as though these differences show that the whole business is false and illusory, a "mere phantasmagoria of men's changing moods"; whereas it may in fact only emphasize once again the personal nature of the reality which is being apprehended and of the act of apprehension itself. And even in the physical world—as Oman has pointed out—it is the real object which presents itself differently to different observers, whereas it is the illusory object, such as a mirage sun or lake, which tends much more to show a flat uniformity.

I propose in the remaining three chapters to set forth one or two of the main elements in the Christian teaching concerning the nature and purpose of the personal God —elements which have been central in the experience and reflection of Christian men and women, though with many individual differences in understanding and exposition, as they have lived in the personal world in the light of God's revelation in Christ. I shall speak of the holiness of God, then of the love of God, and finally of the relation of Christian belief in the love of God to the facts, or what appear to be the facts, of nature and history. I have no intention of trying to say anything new on these matters, even if I were capable of so doing. My purpose rather, as I said at the beginning, is so to present, if I can, acknowledged Christian truth that we are in some measure given a fresh grasp of the deep and consistent personalism of the Christian doctrine of God, and so perhaps may be able the more effectively to present it in our preaching and teaching.

First, then, the holiness of God.

# I

The reason why we take this up first is important, and to understand it will prepare the way for grasping what we have in mind when we speak of God's holiness. The reason is this: Up to this point we have spoken a great deal about God's being personal, about his having created us persons, about his having set us in a world of personal relationships with himself and with one another; that indeed has been our one main topic. Now there is danger in this. The danger is that we bring God, the ultimate source of all there is, right down to our own level. Indeed, there have always been critics of Christianity who say that to think of God as personal at all *is* to bring him right down to our own level in a childish and immature way; it is, they say, a quite crude anthropomorphism, a quite crude thinking of God after the image and similitude of a man.

Well, that it is possible to think of the personal God in a crude and immature way I am not in the least concerned to deny. Though, even so, it is worth pointing out that if God is indeed personal—and I do not know that there is any conclusive reason why he should not in fact be so[1]—then to think of God as such in a crude and immature way would be much nearer the truth than to think of him as an impersonal "It," even if the "It" is expanded, in the pantheistic way, to include everything that exists. But in point of fact mature

[1] That there are theoretical difficulties in the ascription of personality to God is of course true. It is beside my purpose here to enter upon a discussion of them. I will only state my conviction that these difficulties, great as they may be, are not more than difficulties; they do not amount to "conclusive reasons against." Our attitude to them depends in part, I suppose, on the angle from which we approach the matter. If we are merely seeking a theoretical interpretation of the universe, and if the idea of the personal God is to us merely one abstract, theoretical possibility among others, we may feel that the difficulties of the latter are so great as to make it not worth while to pursue it further. But if the truth of the Christian view, with its radical personalism, has laid hold of us, then the theoretical difficulties in the notion of the personal God will be something to wrestle with, but not something to justify the rejection of that notion. In short, the personal nature of God will be *datum*, and not merely theoretical possibility, and the difficulty of conceiving it will be part of the mystery of God.

Christian thought never has apprehended God as personal in a *merely* human way, even though it has maintained that man as personal is made in the divine image, and that God has disclosed his character and purpose toward human persons in the human person of Jesus Christ. Nobody who knew anything about the history of Christian doctrine, or knew anything about what happens in the minds of Christian people when they worship, could ever make such a suggestion. Those who make it merely illustrate once again the way in which some critics of Christianity really do not know what they are talking about.

Nevertheless, in our thought of God as personal the danger of bringing him in a wrong way down to our own level is certainly a real one, and it is most necessary to guard ourselves against it by keeping within the circle of mature Christian thought and experience as these express themselves both in worship and in doctrine. Such Christian thought and experience are protected from that danger by an apprehension of God which can be verbally expressed only in a paradoxical form— an apprehension which, I believe, rests upon God's own self-disclosure to the human spirit. The paradox is this: Christianity affirms that, while God has bestowed upon us a real community of being with himself, in that he has made us to be persons and has personal relationships with us, nevertheless it is also true that he is "wholly other" than we are; he is "wholly other" because he is God, and we are not God, we are men.

Verbally, I repeat, this sounds like self-contradiction;

it sounds like saying that God is wholly other and not wholly other at the same time. And if anybody heartily dislikes even the appearance of contradiction, no doubt some other and more elaborate form of words could be found to express more unexceptionably what is intended —in a sense the remainder of this chapter will be an attempt to express it in other and more elaborate words. But personally I like the astringency of a formula which says in effect that God is wholly other and yet not wholly other at the same time. I use the word "astringency" advisedly; for the word "astringent" in our tongue has come to mean both something that binds together and something that is sharp and challenging to the taste. In worship—that deep and total response of the soul of man to the reality of God—the awareness of God as wholly other and the awareness of him as not wholly other, as near to us and yet very far from us, are fused together without any sense of contradiction whatsoever; yet they are not so fused together that either is lost sight of in the other, for to lose sight of either is immediately to lose the sharp and distinctive flavor—the astringency—of Christian worship. The far God is yet near, the near God is yet far. The "wholly other" is yet "not wholly other," for he has put us in a personal world with himself; the "not wholly other" is yet "wholly other," for he is God, and no other being is, or ever can be, God. And his "wholly other–ness" is discerned as always an integral part of his "not wholly other–ness," and his "not wholly other–ness" is discerned as always an integral part of his "wholly other–ness." The "wholly other–ness" of God is like another range of being of unfathomable depth disclosing itself to us through the more familiar relationships of personal life in which God has been pleased to set us, and through which he gives us kinship with himself.

What is the connection of all this with the "holiness" of God? The connection is this: By the holiness of God we designate everything in his nature and being which constitutes him wholly other than ourselves; we mean, if I may so put it, the sheer incommensurate "God-ness" of God. I like the word "holy" to express this rather than the phrase "wholly other" because it is more familiar and because it connects it more naturally with the act of worship—I suspect that only to those who know, or will come to know, what worship is will what I am saying be any other than a mere juggling with terms. In worship we would not normally say, "O wholly other, yet not wholly other!" but rather, "Holy! holy! holy!" It is true that to most people the first thing the word "holy" suggests, when used of God, is his utterly flawless and pure goodness or righteousness—and that is certainly a centrally important and quite indispensable element in what we mean by the term—but there is no doubt that to define it thus in exclusively ethical terms does less than justice to what the word expresses in that obeisance of the soul of man before God which is worship. By "holiness," then, we mean the sheer, unfathomable, wholly other "God-ness" of God—disclosed to us even through that "not wholly other–ness" of personal being which alone makes it possible for him to disclose anything to us as persons at all.

This holiness, then, this "wholly other–ness" of God thus disclosed to the soul of man, the Christian mind has usually tried to express in its doctrine of God through the words creator, omnipotent, omniscient, omnipresent, eternal, infinitely perfect and glorious. Let us take each of these terms in turn and observe how there enters into the meaning of each of them the two elements of which we have been speaking. We shall observe, first, that the terms have meaning to our minds only because they indicate a relationship into which God enters with our world and because that relationship is reflected in our nature as personal. Then, second, we shall observe that there also enters into the meaning of each the element of "wholly other–ness"—that which makes it distinctively an attribute of the holy God, a manifestation of his "God-ness." From this it will appear how far— how very far—from mere anthropomorphism mature Christian thought has always been in its fearless application of personal terms to God.

## II

First, then, God as *creator*. Creativeness is obviously a very central function of our life as persons; associated with it are some of the deepest satisfactions of which our nature is capable; without it in one form or another our mental life becomes a morass of boredom, stagnation, and decay. And into creative action there enter thought and knowledge; the apprehension of something as having value, as being worthy of existence; and the convergence and focusing of these in an activity sustained by deliberate intention and will—in short, nearly all the distinctive functions of personal life. The thing we create comes into existence because we value it and because we will it, and it would not come into existence at that particular point in space and time apart from that valuing and willing, apart from our deliberate act of creation.

Now when we turn to the Christian apprehension of God as creator, we find that the thought could have no meaning to us at all except in the light of our creativity as persons. As such it enters into, and expresses, once again the intensely personalistic view of God and men which we have repeatedly insisted is so characteristic of the Christian faith. When we say that God is creator of the world and of ourselves, we mean that it and ourselves exist because of God's personal will and deed; it is, in fact, another way of saying that in this universe personal will is primary. Or, to put it negatively, it is a way of rejecting once and for all any notion that the world somehow is God, or even a bit of God, or a sort of unconscious emanation from God like the filament from the belly of a spider, or a by-product of some procreant life force which has no awareness of what it is doing or where it is going. No. The world is in existence, and we are in existence, because God in the fullest possible sense of the term intended it and us. It and we are the result of personal act; it and we are the result of personal will; it and we are the deed of the personal God.

But observe, on the other hand, how there has always entered into the Christian apprehension of the creativity of God the element of unfathomable "wholly other-ness," the fourth dimension, or range of being, of which we spoke, making it distinctively the creativity of *God,* excluding at once any suggestion that in so thinking we are being merely anthropomorphic. Plainly our own creativity is very limited after all; there is in it nothing in the nature of absolute creation. We must be given the materials with which to work, and we must submit to their nature as given; we cannot call them into existence as we will and when we will—the sculptor must have stone, the painter canvas and pigments. But God in his creative activity cannot be thought of as merely working with material which is already there prior to and independently of himself, and to which he must submit. For if that were so, he would not be God, the sole, primary reality; there would be another primary reality not derived from the divine will, but providing the stuff upon which the divine creativity can only get to work. That would be anthropomorphism with a vengeance, a turning of God into a magnified Rembrandt working with messy tubes and smelly oils.

Such a thought the Christian mind has always firmly rejected by attributing to God an absolute creativity, or, as it is sometimes called—in a not very happy phrase—"creation out of nothing." Everything, in strictest and completest literality, depends on him, is given its being by his will. That, of course, is utterly mysterious and quite unimaginable, because there is no parallel to it in our experience. It is part of the "wholly other–ness," without which God would just not be God but only an enlarged replica of ourselves; but taken up into the awareness of God in worship and related to what we do know of creativity as personal act, it is not, I submit—despite its mystery—meaningless nonsense. To say that God *created* all things, and then to add—if we care to use the phrase—"out of nothing," is to comprehend once again in a single astringent formula the transcendent otherness of God, and yet also his essential nature as personal, active will—that will upon which the world and man absolutely depend for their existence and meaning.

### III

Next, God as *omnipotent, omniscient, omnipresent.* I take these three thoughts together, for a reason that will appear as we go on. All three words, once again, have meaning to us at all, only because something of what they indicate is reflected in our own experience as persons having will and purpose. We know what it is to exercise power, to act effectively, to accomplish what we will to accomplish; just as we know what it is to be powerless, to act ineffectively, to be frustrated in respect of what we will and desire. We know too that in so far as we act personally and not merely instinctively—like, say, a grub building a cocoon—effective action depends on knowledge, whereas ineffective action is the fruit of ignorance; a personal will might be defined as an entity which acts, or is capable of acting, through knowledge. We know, further, that effective action in relation to the world requires not merely theoretical observation or knowledge of the world but some sort of causal entry into it, some sort of linkage with its causal connections and sequences. We must in some sense be "there," actually in the arena of events and not merely in the stalls or balcony of comtemplative or wishful thinking.

Turning now to the Christian thought of God: In strict accordance with its profound sense of him as personal, Christian belief apprehends him also under the notions of effectiveness, knowledge, and active presence—yes, but because he is God, the qualifying prefix "omni-" is immediately added in each case. Thus, first, the divine personal will is declared to be omnipotent, that is, omni-effective, wholly competent to achieve its ends. If it were not, God would not be master in his own created world, that is to say, not God. It would mean that there is some reality successfully resistant to God's will and therefore grounded in something other than God's will; it would mean that God is not one to whom man can commit himself in that complete trust which God claims from him.

It is surprising, by the way, how otherwise intelligent people sometimes overlook this point—namely, that the divine omnipotence must be understood strictly in terms of the divine personal will and its intrinsic character and direction. Omnipotence means only that he is wholly competent to achieve what he wills and intends; it does not mean that he can do anything that any clever person likes to think up. To silly conundrums such as whether God, being omnipotent, can tie a knot that he cannot untie the only right answer has always been—and it is not an evasion—"We are not interested." What we are interested in, and it is all we are interested in, is that

God should be competent to achieve what he wills to achieve, not what any sprightly mind may care to suggest.

Of course all this leaves as yet quite unspecified what the intrinsic character of the divine will is, and therefore what he actually does do, or may be expected to do, especially in the realm of persons. Christianity has some very important things to say about that, as we shall see when we come to speak in the next chapter of the love of God.

God, then, is omnipotent, in the sense of omni-competent, omni-effective. Then, second, this combined with the strict adherence to the thought of God as personal will, carries with it for the Christian mind the idea that he is also omniscient. Action according to knowledge, we have said, is the mark of personal action, and the complete effectiveness of God's personal will over the whole of his creation presupposes and implies complete knowledge of the whole of his creation. And, third, and for the same reason, omni-presence is involved. If God's personal will effectively comprehends the whole of his creation, then, in a very real sense, he is relevantly present in all situations whatsoever. You cannot find any spot where his will is not the final determining reality, with which, therefore, in the end all accounts must be settled.

But now observe how all this once again confronts us with the sheer otherness of God, the transcendent "Godness" of God. We cannot comprehend a personal will which holds this vast, complex universe in such an all-inclusive grasp of knowledge and effective action; it utterly eludes our understanding. Yet since we are ourselves personal, set in a personal world with God, the notions of omnipotence, omnipresence and omniscience are not meaningless—far from it. They comprise at one and the same time the transcendent mystery of his being, and yet also his nature disclosed to us as personal. Perhaps the best way to realize that these great thoughts of God are not meaningless, though they baffle understanding—one way, too, to get away from the dullness and deadness of the merely abstract statement we have been making—is to come at them once again through the personal relationship in which we ourselves stand to God, and through which God reveals himself to us.

It is difficult to believe that anybody could be so completely devoid of a direct sense of God that he does not feel something of the solemnizing challenge of, say, the 139th psalm—does not feel, that is, its *meaningfulness*, for without meaning it could not so move us and challenge us. The psalm is a religious meditation—as distinguished from an abstract philosophical analysis and discussion—on the omniscience, omnipresence, and creative power of God. It springs out of the heart of the personal relationship through which the personal God approaches, and claims, and discloses his being and character to men; as such it is filled both with clear conviction and with an awed and worshipful sense of the mystery of it all. Omniscience:

O Lord, thou hast searched me, and known me.
Thou knowest my downsitting and mine uprising, thou
    understandest my thought afar off.

Thou compassest my path and my lying down, and art acquainted with all my ways.

For there is not a word in my tongue, but, lo, O Lord, thou knowest it altogether.

Omnipresence:

Thou hast beset me behind and before, and laid thine hand upon me.

Such knowledge is too wonderful for me; it is high, I cannot attain unto it.

Whither shall I go from thy spirit? or whither shall I flee from thy presence?

If I ascend up into heaven, thou art there: if I make my bed in hell, behold, thou art there.

If I take the wings of the morning, and dwell in the uttermost parts of the sea;

Even there shall thy hand lead me, and thy right hand shall hold me.

Creation:

Thou hast possessed my reins: thou hast covered me in my mother's womb.

I will praise thee; for I am fearfully and wonderfully made: marvellous are thy works; and that my soul knoweth right well.

My substance was not hid from thee, when I was made in secret, and curiously wrought in the lowest parts of the earth.

Thine eyes did see my substance, yet being unperfect; and in thy book all my members were written, which in continuance were fashioned, when as yet there was none of them.

The inference from God's knowing all about me, from God's being always present with me wherever I am and whatever I do, and from God's having made me, to God's knowing all about everything, to God's being present everywhere, and to God's having made all things, is indeed not a logical one; but we are not here in the realm of discursive thought. We are here in the realm of the direct self-disclosure of God to the soul in a way that is both meaningful, being of a person to a person, and beyond comprehension, being of God. How firmly the whole thing is held within the context of the personal encounter of God with man in absolute claim upon him is shown by the words with which the psalm concludes: "Search me, O God, and know my heart: try me and know my thoughts: and see if there be any wicked way in me."

## IV

Third, God as *eternal*. What is meant by this?

We begin again in the sphere of our own distinctive experience as persons, and we note the following significant fact about it: As finite persons we are immersed in the time process—all our experience comes to us under the form of a time sequence of events, under the form of past, present, and future. Nevertheless—even while we stand within it and cannot get out of it—we do in some measure stand over against it and above it. For we can in some measure grasp and anticipate the future before it happens—indeed by foresight and planning we can creatively cause to happen what otherwise would not happen—and we can in some measure grasp the past, after it has happened, in memory and recollection. Moreover, it is precisely in this strange power to stand over against and above the series of events, to grasp both past and future in the present through memory and imagination, that nearly all our distinctive prerogative as personal beings with responsible wills is rooted. Take the power away and at once we cease to be persons, capable of personal relationships. Our awareness of ourselves as selves persisting throughout all the changes of the years, our growth in knowledge and wisdom, our sense of moral responsibility, our capacities for undeviating love and loyalty to friends, everything distinctively personal is found, when you analyze it, to rest at one point or another on this power over time—to rest on what Carlyle called the mystic faculties of memory and hope, through which "thou, even thou, the earth-blinded, summonest both past and future and communest with them."

Yet this power over time is after all very limited. Our personal memory is very short and patchy, and our power to anticipate and shape the future is very restricted. We are continually frustrated by the unforeseen and the unpredictable, and this is particularly so in the realm of personal relations, the realm of history, for there we are in the world of freedom, of beings who in their own inaccessible interior life are beyond the reach of our control. And over all hangs the ever-present possibility, and the final certainty, of death; in death the transience of time seems finally to engulf the self-conscious person himself, to engulf that one being in its midst who has been conscious of it as transient, and has in some degree stood above it—who has grasped the flux of events and, if only for a period and in a limited degree, has deliberately and consciously controlled its movement.

It is some evidence of this contradictory situation in which we as persons find ourselves in the midst of the time process that we yearn at one and the same time both for the abiding and for the ever-changing, for the permanent and for the transitory. Sensitive minds which have gone some way on life's journey feel deeply, and less sensitive minds feel at least occasionally, the sad transiency of things, "time's remorselessly corroding tooth," the pathos of the days, the scenes, the hopes, the persons, that are no more. Yet on the other hand nothing irks us so much as the permanent, the unchanging, the monotonous; it is the very definition of boredom. Thus, as persons, and only because we are persons, we live in two elements at once. We are in time yet, partially at least, above it; we are masters of it yet in the end apparently mastered by it.

Now set all this in the context of the Christian apprehension of God. Once again, in accordance with its profound sense of him as personal, active will encountering us and claiming us in history, it insists that time, history, has the utmost significance for God even as it has for us. God is in some real sense at work in it; he acts in it, or, perhaps we should say, into it. He acts in it, or into it, supremely through Jesus Christ. Nevertheless, because he is the *divine* person, he must be above it, master of it—yet not relatively, patchily, frustratedly, for a brief period, like human persons, but absolutely. For if he were not absolute master of it, he would once more not be God; his will would not be "omni-effective" in it.

Thus the distinctive Christian understanding of the eternity of God comes into view. It does not mean—as popular thought sometimes supposes it to mean—that God is immersed in the time series as we are, the only difference being that he is not subject to death and so goes on for ever and ever; that would be a very crude anthropomorphism. Nor does it mean what Greek thought tended to make it mean—namely, that God in his essential being as eternal has nothing to do with time at all, but dwells wholly above and beyond and apart from it; so that time is unreal to God, and the only way for us to have communion with him is to escape from it altogether, or as much as possible, through trance or ecstatic vision, or in some other way. No, he is at work in the time process; its events have meaning for him; and we as finite persons immersed in it can have full fellowship with him in responding to his claim and doing his will. Nevertheless he is absolute master of the time process; he is above it in the fullest sense, for he has created it, has its every event within the knowledge and control of his manifold wisdom, and can bring it to an end when his work in it is completed and his will accomplished.

All of this defies our understanding. It is not possible for us to think in any other than temporal terms, and the mode of being of one who is eternal, and yet to whom time is significant, the sphere of purposive action, is utterly beyond us. Nevertheless the mystery is not, I submit, a mystery of complete meaninglessness. It has meaning to us because God has given us personal being in a finite mode, so that we ourselves in some measure stand above the mere procession of events; and, even more, because through his dealings with us as personal beings he continually discloses to us both his nature as personal and also at the same time his transcendent otherness as God.

## V.

Finally, the *infinite perfection and glory* of God.

Once again we begin with our distinctive experience as persons, and in particular with that aspect of it to which reference has already been made, namely, creativity. Creativity, broadly interpreted, might be regarded as in some sense a mark of all sentient existence—the birds build nests, the beavers make dams—but in human experience it becomes, or can become, something entirely different from such purely instinctive creativity in the interests of merely biological needs. It becomes in fact distinctively personal; it becomes, that is to say, the deliberate endeavor to bring into existence things or situations because we *judge* them to be good and worthy of existence, and because, having so judged, we acknowledge that we *ought* to bring them into existence. The element of self-conscious will and of moral valuation enters in. It will, I think, be generally acknowledged that in this capacity to recognize ourselves to be under the claim of ideal values—usually comprehended in the formula "the true, the beautiful, and the good"—much of our distinctive nature as persons consists, whatever view

138

may be taken as to its wider philosophical implications.

Now the Christian view takes this aspect of personal life as we know it right up into its doctrine of God. As we saw earlier,[2] it affirms that in the claim of ideal values there encounters the will of man none other than the creative will of the personal God himself, calling man to be a personal fellow worker with him in the actualization of the true, the beautiful, and the good in history. Only by rightly responding to this call can the true purpose of man's life as a finite person be fulfilled.

Yet for the Christian view this is not enough, for it might be held to be consonant with the notion, which some have held, of a finite and struggling God, who is just another personal seeker after the good along with ourselves, even though on a higher plane. Such a thought of God is utterly repugnant to the Christian mind—it is much too anthropomorphic; it lacks the note of the "wholly other." It in effect denies once again that God is the sole ultimate reality, from whose creative will *all* things depend and draw their being, and to whom we can *wholly* commit ourselves in obedience and trust; for it implies that there is some other realm of being over against, and higher than, God—some source or reservoir of ideal values which is, so to say, beyond him, and which he is seeking to appropriate and express along with us.

Furthermore such a thought of God repudiates that living apprehension of him which lies at the heart of worship, namely, that his is an infinite and inexhaustible richness of being which comprehends within itself all perfection and utterly transcends the highest reach not only of man but also of any other type of being, however exalted—whether angel or archangel—he has made. God is the sole reality worthy of worship, and in the worship of him alone all created personal beings find their completion and perfection. For the true worshiper even that best righteousness which God himself bestows, and enables man to receive, remains, and must remain, "filthy rags"; nor would he have it otherwise. For to apprehend the infinite perfection of God, to be humbled and yet also continually uplifted and enlarged by it, to seek after it and to receive of it within the present limits of our life, knowing that there will always be more to seek and to receive, no matter how much those limits may be expanded by the seeking and receiving—all this is the highest distinction of that finite personal life which God the infinite person has bestowed upon us, as it is also the source of its greatest joy. It is God who says, "Ask, and go on asking, and ye shall always receive; seek, and go on seeking, and ye shall always find; knock, and go on knocking, and it shall always be opened unto you"; and he is able to give this assurance because all perfection is already comprehended within the infinite richness of his own underived being.

Obviously there is mystery enough here; obviously this is no childishly anthropomorphic picture of the personal God. Knowing, as we do, only the search and partial attainment, we are baffled to comprehend what that mode of being must be which has within itself an infinite and fully realized perfection. We are in the presence of the

140

"wholly other" than ourselves. Nevertheless it is not a meaningless "wholly other"; on the contrary, as apprehended through the highest moments of worshipful adoration and in creative seeking and obedience, it is full of meaning, rightly claiming—if it does not receive—a man's uttermost devotion. Thus the Bible, which speaks from beginning to end quite simply of God as personal, speaks with equal simplicity—as though either a human person will know what it means or, if he does not, there is no means of telling him unless God himself breaks through the darkness of his soul—of his glory.

There is, however, a further thing to be said; it takes us right to the heart of the distinctive Christian doctrine of God. It may well be asked why God, if he already has within himself an infinite richness and perfection of being, has created a race of finite persons—persons who must learn, in the freedom and within the limits of their finite personal life, to share that richness. Does not that imply that there was something lacking in his being which God had to set about supplying?

In the end this also must run out into mystery, as all our questionings concerning God must—just because God is God. Nevertheless the Christian faith has some light to shed on this mystery also. For it bids us believe that God's will to create finite persons in order that they may share his life does not imply a defect in the divine perfection but rather expresses the deepest and most central thing in that perfection. How so? Because, whatever else may be comprehended in the unfathomable perfection of his being, the deepest and most central thing in that perfection is his love. The bringing into existence of finite persons to share together in his life is an outflowing of the divine nature as love. To use a phrase of Brunner's, God creates men out of love and for love. Thus, in Christian thought, the personal nature of God and his infinite glory—which might otherwise make the personal as we know it seem quite insignificant—are firmly held together. The creation and love of persons are part of his infinite glory—indeed, the highest part, if such distinctions in respect of the infinite are permissible—the infinite glory of the omnipresent, omnipotent, omniscient, eternal, yet always personal God.

# THE LOVE OF GOD

IT MIGHT reasonably be maintained that in all that I have set forth concerning God's holiness there was nothing peculiarly Christian—nothing, that is to say, springing from the distinctively Christian assertion of God's great and final act of self-disclosure and self-giving into the midst of the human personal world in Jesus Christ. Certainly long before Christ came, the Old Testament writers spoke of God as holy, in the sense in which we have expounded that word; and certainly it is still possible to believe in God's holiness in that sense without in the least committing oneself to the distinctive Christian belief concerning Jesus Christ, or to any statements about God which that belief might be held to imply; many in fact do so.

If, then, we ask what *is* the quite distinctive Christian doctrine of God's nature and purpose, as disclosed in Jesus Christ, the answer will be found in the doctrine that he is love. Yet—and this is the point I am now wanting to emphasize—this distinctive Christian doctrine of love of God, which we are now going to examine, must be kept firmly in the context of the divine holiness which we have already considered. There must be no separation between the two doctrines. Whenever we begin to think of God under the aspect of his love, we are always in special danger of bringing him down to the level of our small human selves, of trivializing and cheapening him in immature and childish anthropomorphisms, of losing hold of what we called the sheer "God-ness" of God.

This danger has at least three sources. The first is to be found in the many meanings which the term "love" can bear in English; the effect of this is that when the word is used by different people in discussion, they imagine they are thinking and talking about the same thing when in fact they are not doing so at all.

The second is that when we think of God as love, we instantly bring him, as it were, into the most intimate texture of our own personal existence. This puts us under constant temptation to think of God in a much too direct and uncritical way, after the image of our own personal relationships with one another. This temptation does not arise in connection with words like omnipotent, omniscient, omnipresent; in these terms the "otherness" of God lies, as it were, much nearer the surface, and can hardly be missed. None of us is likely to think of himself as omnipotent or omniscient or omnipresent but it is easy to think that we know well enough what it means to love and be loved.

The third source of danger lies in the fact that the thought of God as love, so to say, centralizes us as persons in the perspective of the divine will. To say that God loves us is certainly to say that we are of the highest importance to him; but this at once lays the truth of the divine love peculiarly open to the distortions of our sinful minds. For, as we saw earlier, it is precisely our egocen-

religious ideas of mankind. That is undoubtedly true so far as the mere use of the term is concerned. God is referred to in the Old Testament as the Father of Israel, and there are places where his fatherly tenderness is described in moving words. And even pagan writers refer to God as Father. Homer, for example, describes Zeus as the father of men; and in primitive religions the same idea certainly appears.

But obviously the mere use of the same term does not amount to much, though, I suppose, it could be argued that such widespread usage shows that there is in the hearts of men at least a dim apprehension of the truth of the matter. Everything, in fact, depends on the content put into the term, and the extent to which such content is able to grip and re-create the lives of men, to regulate and interpret their experience over its whole breadth, especially those elements in their experience which seem to make mockery of such a belief. The more I study the New Testament, in the context of the general history of religions, the more clear it becomes that the thought of God as fatherly love as this is revealed in the whole life and death of Jesus Christ—even more than in his teaching—*is* unique in its content, its profundity, its consistency, its challenge, its austerity, its power to enter formatively and creatively and in a self-authenticating way into the lives of men.

In passing we may say that nothing could be more superficial than the methods of some critics, who unearth parallels to fragments of Christ's teaching about God from other writings of the same—or a previous—period and suppose that by so doing they have finally disposed of any claim to uniqueness that may be made on Christ's behalf. As I once heard it put, doubtless at the time of the Trojan war there were some women with eyes as beautiful as Helen's, and others with hair as beautiful as Helen's, and others again with complexion as beautiful as Helen's; but there was only one Helen who united beauty of eyes, hair, complexion, and all the rest into one glorious harmony of beauty, and "launched a thousand ships." There is, I repeat, no setting forth of God as fatherly love which is in the least degree comparable, in its reach and depth and undiminished creative and re-creative power, with that which comes to us from the whole personal being of Jesus, his words and deeds, his life and death. And after all, only Jesus Christ has launched—without any exercise of force and coercion—the "thousand ships" of the Christian Church.

The other suggestion which is disposed of by the New Testament thought of God as the Father of our Lord Jesus Christ is the suggestion which is sometimes made by those who add a smattering of knowledge of Christianity to a smattering of knowledge of psychology—and how common these mixed smatterings are today! It is maintained that belief in God as Father is never anything more than a fantasy product of weak souls—of weak souls who, feeling their inadequacy in face of life, and desperately wanting the support and protection of a beneficent power greater than themselves, revert unconsciously to their early childhood and take refuge in the imaginary arms of a great big celestial "daddy." It would be superfluous and out of place to discuss such a theory here—it has often enough been dealt with in other places.[1] As I have already indicated, I am not in the least concerned to deny that such disreputable mental processes are in ever-present danger, needing to be kept in check. My point is simply that nobody who had taken the trouble to enter at all deeply into the picture of God as Father given us through Jesus Christ could suppose that it was, or is, the mere fantasy product of feeble and half-defeated souls. The picture is much too austere, searching, demanding for that—it is, in fact, such that no weak soul would ever want to seek refuge in it.

Let us try now to set forth some of the central elements in this austere and searching picture of the fatherly love of the personal God as given us through Christ and the New Testament, even at the risk of saying what to some of us may seem trite and obvious. For certainly if our gospel is to have any convincing and regenerative power at all in this grim modern world, we must at all costs dispel the cloud of sentimentalism which has come to surround this central affirmation of the divine love; we must at all costs avoid giving the impression that Christian teaching in the modern world is little more than the spraying of rose water on a stableyard.

## I

The first and most fundamental truth is that God's will of love is directed always to the *fashioning of finite persons into worthy sonship to himself*. God's purpose with men

---

[1] As, for example, in my own *Towards Belief in God* (1942) , pp. 168 ff.

is that they should, under the conditions set by their finite earthly life as persons, have personal fellowship with himself—the condition of that fellowship being that they should will what he wills, value what he values, in short, be *good* persons according to the pattern of his own goodness. "Be ye therefore perfect," says Christ, "even as your Father which is in heaven is perfect"; Paul speaks of the creation's waiting "for the manifestation of the sons of God"; the writer to the Hebrews speaks of God's "bringing many sons unto glory."

That God's purpose should be conceived to be thus wholly directed toward making men *good* sons may perhaps, once again, sound a trifle soft; in our speech the word "good" as applied to persons—like the word "love" —is apt to have some sentimental overtones. It hints at the goody-goody. "Be good, sweet maid, and let who will be clever." But this only witnesses once again to the necessity of reinterpreting our terms in accordance with the revelation in Christ. Clearly, so reinterpreted, this is as far from being a sentimental truth as anything could be. That God intends above all things else that men shall be good is in fact a very solemn and startling truth; it introduces at once a note of severity into the loving purpose of God and his dealings with men. It cuts right across the hedonism of the natural man. It means that men have not been put into this world primarily in order to enjoy themselves. It means that God does not ever order men's lives merely to give them a good time and save them from trouble. On the contrary, the love of God is ready to put men through severe disciplines in order that they may learn to participate in that wherein alone the true blessedness of personal life is to be found, namely, in the doing of his will as sons.

It should be observed that I have just used the word "blessedness." It is an important word and I have chosen it deliberately. It would be wrong to take out of what I have just said the idea that according to Christian faith God has *no* interest whatever in men's being happy; that would be absurd. What Christian belief does say is that there is in the nature of things a condition attached to the achievement of happiness, a condition which God himself could ignore only by negating himself. The condition is that men should do his will. And furthermore, and much more important—for indeed it is obvious enough, altogether apart from Christianity, that happiness in this world is not to be had merely for the asking— the Christian faith, in accordance with the revelation in Christ, reinterprets and greatly deepens the notion of happiness, so much so that we have to find another word for it, such as the word "blessedness." The New Testament says frankly that the doing of God's will may involve a man in experiences which are most grievous and burdensome, but that nevertheless because he is walking humbly with God there will be—underlying and permeating them—a peace and a victory which go far, far deeper than merely happy feelings. God's purpose, then, is not primarily to make men happy; it is to make them good, and so to give them *blessedness,* in the doing of his will.

It is hardly necessary to illustrate this note of austerity from the Gospels themselves. Leaving on one side the fact that the life therein depicted as wholly surrendered to the will of God issued in an anguish of suffering so great that it was supportable at all only because it had at its heart the incommunicable blessedness of such dedication, there are sayings enough whose severity is veiled from us only by their familiarity. "If thy hand offend thee, cut it off"; "If thine eye offend thee, pluck it out"; "It is better . . . to enter into life maimed than . . . to go into hell." Jesus tells his would-be followers again and again, particularly when they flock after him in excited crowds, that they are in for stern times if they link their wills with the divine will; but he also tells them that they are in for stern times if they do not, the difference being that in the one case the sternness leads on to something infinitely worth while, whereas in the other case it leads on to nothing except ruin and despair. Upon all human habitations there beat storms and floods—God has provided no easy way, no short cuts to happiness, for any of us—but the house built on the rock of the divine will stands, whereas the house which is not so built tumbles down, and great is its ruin. This is certainly no milk-and-water view of the fatherly love of God; it is stark realism; and it accords with facts.

## II

Second, God's fashioning of men into worthy sonship to himself is *always through freedom and for freedom*. This is of course but to say, again, that God's dealings with men are always in the last resort personal, and never *merely* manipulative and overriding. I say "in the last resort" and "never *merely* manipulative" because Christian truth does not call upon us to think that God, in the complex wisdom and patience of his dealings with men, *never* makes any sort of entry into their lives of which they are not aware and to which therefore, at the moment, they cannot relate themselves in a fully personal way. We must concede God the right to use, both through the interior access he has to men's souls—and has wisely denied to us—and in other ways, the plasticity which he himself has put into human nature; but the point is, if I may so put it, that he can be trusted never to use it wrongly, as we so often do in our own sinful dealings with one another. In all his dealings with men there will remain a central sanctuary of freedom which under no circumstances whatever will he violate. Never will he, so to say, machine-stamp men into what he desires them to be; always in the last resort a man must respond through his own illumined insight, and with the consent of his own will.

We have already spoken a great deal throughout this study of this central and indispensable aspect of the personal world, as distinct from the world of things wherein control by manipulation is necessary and in order. The point now is that Christian teaching, if it is to be true to the revelation in Christ, must take this respect for freedom right up into its doctrine of God and of his dealings with men.

It is impressive indeed to mark with what consistency this note of respect for freedom does enter into the mind and teaching of Jesus Christ. There is the often-repeated saying, "He that hath ears to hear, let him hear"—the truth must be presented, and the individual must hear and respond. There is his use of parable, part of the purpose of which seems to have been to elicit the hearer's own insight into God's purpose as this meets and challenges him in the daily situations of his life, in the events of the time, and particularly in Christ's own coming. There is his whole method of teaching and preparing his disciples—a study in itself—and, at the end, his commitment of his whole cause to them with little or nothing of precise instruction or planned organization.

In the fulfillment of his own vocation as the bearer and revealer of God's saving purpose in the world he decisively rejected once and for all the plan—attractive as it must have been to one so virile and so superbly equipped—to compel men's allegiance to himself by some portentous display of power; this the story of the Temptation makes clear. More than once he was asked to provide a sign from heaven to put the truth of his claims beyond doubt; he steadfastly refused to do so. "You are able to interpret the signs of the weather," he said in effect on one occasion; "why cannot you of your own selves judge what is right and read the signs of the times?" He was asked by his disciples to call down fire from heaven upon an inhospitable Samaritan village; he sternly rebuked them, saying, "Ye know not what manner of spirit ye are of." He believed that the whole power of God was with him in the work he was sent to do; in that sense he could say that twelve legions of angels were at his disposal; but such power, he knew, was not to be exercised in the way that the unregenerate minds of men would naturally associate with such a metaphor—that is to say, through a display of coercive and overriding might. Therefore, in that sense at least, he would not call upon angels to assist him, even when he was in the power of his enemies. The readiness to go to Calvary was itself a final and decisive repudiation of any thought that God could or would seek to overcome the evil in men's hearts by such methods.

All of this sounds, even as one says it, somewhat trite and obvious. Nevertheless it is most necessary that it should be said. If we are to enter into the truth of the Christian revelation and to discover in increasing degree its self-authenticating power, it is most important to make up our minds to take really seriously this patient respect on the part of God for the freedom of his children.

It is most important for at least two reasons. The first is that the bias of our minds is set in precisely the opposite direction. I have referred to this more than once already. It is part of our sinful blindness to the true order of the personal world that we are always wanting short cuts with people; we are possessed with the will to power—"power" being interpreted fundamentally in terms of overriding force and control. And though we pay lip service to the ideal of freedom, deep down we are, far more than we realize, afraid of it. We are afraid of it sometimes even for ourselves, seeking for some infallible authority to direct us what to believe, or what to do—an infallible book, an infallible church, an infallible orthordoxy, an infallible leader. And we think in the same terms of God. We would like him to lay bare his mighty arm and blast wickedness, or at least the extremer forms of it, from off the face of the earth. We forget that we ourselves would come in for some of the blasting; it is the other man we want blasted. We do not see, unless we continually make the effort to see, that such an exercise of power would be a confession of weakness on the part of God—that is, if God is indeed fatherly love. It would mean, not that he is omnipotent, omnicompetent, but that he is not; it would mean that he is not able to do what in his fatherly love he purposes to do; it would mean that, unable to win men as persons, he can only manipulate them like puppets or swat them like flies.

This brings us to the second reason, which is that if we are not ready thus to rethink our notions of power in relation to God, if we are not prepared—I repeat—to take really seriously the truth that, just because he loves persons, he steadfastly honors their freedom, then it is impossible to get any light at all on the dark suffering and confusion of human history, and in particular on the problem of how, in the face of such confusion and suffering, a man may yet properly be called upon to believe in the goodness of God. I shall return to this again in the last chapter; all I want to say now is that, while of course the Christian revelation does not shed a complete illumination on this dread problem of evil, there is at least some light in the thought that whatever else human history is, it is, in Croce's phrase, " the story of liberty." It is because we do not see that liberty and love go indissolubly together, that we find it so much harder to see how a world like this and a divine overshadowing love can go together. It is most important to grasp the truth that there are evil things that God permits *because* he is love, not because he is not.

## III

Third, God being fatherly love, his austere and free-dom-respecting purpose *never turns aside from, or deserts, any human person that he has made—no matter who he is or into what darkness and corruption of sin he may come.* On the contrary, he seeks with undeviating patience, and at any cost, to bring every man back to that true personal life which is to be found only in fellowship with himself and in the doing of his will. Here we confront the most distinctive truth in the Christian doctrine of the love of God, a truth whose startling originality, so challenging and condemning to all our normal habits of mind, is veiled from us—who have lived in the midst of the Christian tradition—only by its familiarity, though it is still further obscured by the abstractly generalizing sentimentality with which it is not infrequently set forth.

How glibly, sometimes, do we announce that God loves *all* men—how little startled, apparently, by what we are saying! Surely such complacent utterance is possible only because the word "God" does not mean to us the ever-present, active, holy Will with which we ourselves—in every situation, in all *our* dealings with men—must settle accounts; because, too, the word "love" does not mean to us anything more than a vaguely benevolent sentiment of good will; because, most of all, the words "all men," "everybody" are impersonal abstractions lacking all sharp particularity in our minds. It becomes an altogether different proposition when, giving due thought to all its terms, we try to focus it upon someone who has done us bitter and irreparable wrong, or from whom for one reason or another we utterly recoil. Whatever our recoil, it remains true—unless the *distinctively* Christian doctrine of the love of God is wholly false—that God does love, let us say, the commandant of the Belsen concentration camp no less than he loves anybody reading this book —loves him, that is, in the austere sense in which we have been considering its meaning up to this point. Nothing that man—or anybody else—can do, or can become, can take him outside the scope of the undeviating divine purpose of good toward him; nothing whatever can make him worthless in the sight of God.

This unqualified universality of the divine love, which lights on a person simply because he is "there" as a person and not because he has this, that, or the other lovable quality, is so utterly different from anything that we know as love in our human relationships that it has become customary among theologians to use a distinctive term for it. And this is the more necessary because, as I have said, "love" is in English such an ambiguous and even degraded word. The distinctive word is the New Testament Greek word *agape*. Those who know Nygren's classic—if at times somewhat onesided—treatment of this matter [2] will not need to be reminded of the difference between divine love, *agape,* and what we think of as love in our relationship with one another.

With us love is a feeling-attitude or sentiment evoked

[2] *Agape and Eros* (Eng. tr. 1932).

in us by the qualities of a person, or by the fact that he stands in some special relationship to us; we love a person because he has winsome qualities, or because he is our child, or because he has been good to us and generously supplied some need. If he lacks these qualities or, still more, is characterized by their opposite, we do not love him—and, we are ready to add, cannot be expected to love him.

The divine love, according to the New Testament meaning of the term *agape,* is sharply contrasted with this attitude. *Agape* is free, spontaneous, and universal; it is a love which springs from the ultimate being and nature of the personal God, and goes out to every person he has created, irrespective of merit or worth—or, indeed, of any other quality which *we* would consider likely to call forth, or justify, love. So far, indeed, is it from being true that God loves persons because they are valuable that, to be accurate, we must reverse the proposition and say that persons are valuable because God loves them; the love is primary, the value is secondary and derivative. With us, on the other hand, the value—or what we consider to be such—is primary, and the love is derivative and dependent upon that. It is therefore never a complete Christian statement to say that a person has intrinsic value in himself; the complete Christian statement is that a man has value because God—who in his own nature is love—loves him, and loves him for no other reason whatsoever than that he is a man whom God has made.

It is hardly necessary to say that in our task of making clear to our contemporaries this distinctive Christian understanding of the love of God we shall not be able to use the word *agape*. Apart from its strangeness and ugliness, if it frees us from some of the debased associations of the word "love," it also deprives us of its nobler and warmer overtones of meaning and feeling. We shall need to go on using the more familiar word. But that only makes it the more urgent that the quite distinctive nature of the divine love—that which makes it not merely natural human love in an intensified and more universal form, but something radically different, something quite literally *super*natural—should be made unmistakably plain to men, for three reasons at least.

First, because it is only as men can be brought to see the divine love in this its undiscriminating absoluteness and universality that they can be convinced of its reality. Its unmotivated universality, requiring no attractive qualities in a person to call it forth, does not make it unbelievable; rather it is precisely that which makes it believable—as an attribute of God. The doctrine of the divine *agape* is indeed another illustration of the steadfast refusal of Christianity, even when it is thinking of God in radically personal terms, to be merely anthropomorphic; and this refusal, while at the same time, it is keeping unwaveringly in the sphere of the personal, is, I believe, one source of its power over the human heart.

Second, without some vision of the divine love as *agape* no man can even begin to have a deep, sincere, and poignant awareness of his own sinful lovelessness, and of the need for, as well as the wonder of, God's forgiveness. Nowhere is the profound alienation of our minds from

God more clearly shown to us than in the fact that even our highest self-givings in love are in fact so limited in reach and scope, so much under the control of purely natural instincts and desires.

Third, only by emphasizing the essential nondependence of God's love upon the qualities of the person loved can we dispose of the notion that the Christian doctrine of God as love really ascribes to him a weak and sentimental unrealism. It is because we can think of love only as reaching out to a person whose qualities give us some reason for loving him that we imagine that a love which reaches out to a monster like the commandant of the concentration camp can do so only by not seeing him as he really is or by pretending that he is other than he is. The divine lover thus becomes for us the divine dupe or the divine sentimentalist.

This leads me to say a word on the wrath of God, which of course is as much a New Testament thought of him as the thought of his love. It is clear that if we are not permitted to think of God's love after the image of our purely natural affections and emotions, we are certainly not permitted to think of the divine wrath after the image of our purely natural impulses of anger. We must tread warily here. Obviously if we are to speak of God's wrath at all, we must connect it with what was said earlier about the severe and disciplinary side of the divine love. In God's dealings with finite persons there is—there must be—a principle of judgment, a principle of the repudiation and annihilation of sin; a universe grounded in the holy will of God, and suitable for the fashioning of persons into harmony with that will in freedom, is not thinkable on any other terms. Sin must have, and does have, all those frightful consequences of which we spoke in an earlier chapter, and it can be no part of love to protect men from them in a merely soft and indulgent way. Such austere truths, we have insisted, are not alien to the Christian understanding of the love of God, but are rather part of its content. If God is love, then the loveless- ness of men must bring dire results such as we see all about us today; men cannot go against the grain of the universe and not get splinters. The state of the world today does not prove that God is not love; rather it helps to prove that he is.

So far as we wish to guard against any obscuring or minimization of this aspect of the divine love, we may well use the word "wrath," as the New Testament does; but the ever-present danger is, as I have said, that we interpret the word too much after the image of our own anger. Anger with us is very apt to be a merely destructive and sterile emotion, seeking primarily to hurt and destroy the offending person—an emotion which for the time being blinds us to the fact that he never ceases as a person to have an inalterable claim upon us. Some thinkers, feel- ing acutely this danger of transferring our own angry feeling to God—with reflex effects on human behavior of a shocking kind, for it would seem at once to give divine sanction to all sorts of utterly merciless dealing with persons in the name of righteousness—suggest that we should avoid the phrase "the wrath of God" and speak only of the inevitable consequences which must attach themselves to any going against the divine intention and will. But that too has its disadvantages; for if we are not careful, it may subtly depersonalize, mechanize, the whole relationship; it may minimize what is the supremely important fact about sin from the Christian point of view, namely, that it alienates men as persons from the personal God. It suggests that the universe is just a sort of slot machine, which, if we put in our moral pennies, delivers the appropriate piece of chocolate, users of bent coins being liable to the stated fine. The word "wrath" at least keeps this central matter firmly within the sphere of the personal. It is indeed one mark of the mind awakened to the real nature of God, and of the personal world in which God has set us with himself, that it no longer feels the notion of necessary consequence to be by itself quite adequate, but begins to discern, through the suffering and confusion which inevitably overtake wrong-doing, a holy personal Will.

The only thing to do, if we do thus use the word "wrath"—and on the whole we are probably less open to error if we do use it than if we do not—is to be clear in our own minds that by it we are signifying one aspect of the more inclusive truth that God is *agape*. It is part of the continuous outgoing of his *agape* toward persons; it is the inevitable and spontaneous recoil of love from lovelessness, the steadfast setting of itself against it. Wrath is the burning, fiery heart of utterly pure love. It is love as "consuming fire"—never, therefore, separated from the profoundest possible concern over the fact that in the end the most bitter sufferer from sin must be the sinner himself. It is one undivided movement of love such as we in our disintegrated personal life only vaguely comprehend. It is a recoil from the sinner for what he is, and yet a holding onto him—not because of what he is, or even because of what he will be, but because he is "there," a person whom God has made. A man may sin himself into the wrath of God, but never out of his love: that is what *agape* means.

If now we ask what is the source of this Christian apprehension of the love of God as *agape,* running so completely counter to all our instinctive and natural ideas of love, there can be no doubt as to the answer: It springs from Jesus Christ. This is indeed "the God and Father of our Lord Jesus Christ"! It springs from his teaching about God, and about human relationship to God. He symbolizes God's universal, nonselective rule of love by the rain which falls on just and unjust alike, by a father receiving back—indeed going forth to meet, without questions asked or conditions imposed—the returning prodigal; by a shepherd looking for a lost sheep, a woman searching for a lost coin. And righteousness in men, or what they deem to be such, he says, constitutes no claim as of desert upon the love of God, for that love generously reaches out to them irrespective of their deserts; it does not work under the stimulus of desert at all. And for the same reason sin involves no forfeiture of it; righteous men are not loved because of their righteousness, and unrighteous men are not left unloved because of their unrighteousness. And, as for human relationships, these, he teaches, should themselves mirror and express the divine *agape*. Men also must love persons just because they are there—and even the fact that they are enemies must make no difference whatever. It springs, too, from Jesus' own attitude to men and women—Zacchaeus, the woman taken in adultery, Mary Magdalene. What startled and challenged his contemporaries more than anything else was that he received sinners and ate with them. Even the unification of love and wrath is to be discerned in him. He recoiled in anger from the hard cruelties that pious men, even in the name of God, practiced upon one another; yet also he wept over such men, for the weeping over Jerusalem was not over bricks and mortar, but over precisely these people who had slain God's messengers in the past and were now concentrating upon slaying him also. Most of all, it springs from Jesus' understanding and fulfillment of his own vocation as the one sent by God to be the divine *agape* itself in saving action toward sinful men. In accordance with that vocation he must lay down his life on the cross for men; his action in going to Calvary is the embodiment of the divine action, the divine *agape,* in history. "The Son of man," he said, "is come to seek and to save that which was lost—to give his life a ransom for many." [3]

[3] I find myself very reluctant at this point to pass over Christ's atoning work at Calvary without further treatment. Christ's atoning work, it is superfluous to say, has always been central in the Christian experience of God as personal, and gospel; and it has been the subject of profound reflection on the part of Christian thinkers through the centuries. But I have found the subject too vast and deep for the cursory treatment which a study such as this requires. I have chosen to illustrate my main theme by some aspects of the Christian doctrine of God, and to that I had better adhere. It is perhaps sufficient to say that the profundity of the Christian doctrine of forgiveness through the Cross of Christ matches the profundity of its doctrine of sin, and that even as its radical personalism is manifest—as we saw—in the latter, so also it is manifest

## IV

There is, finally, a fourth element in the distinctively Christian conception of the divine fatherly love, as this is given to us through Christ and the New Testament. It is that, while the love of God lights upon the individual —and in so doing bestows indefeasible value on him— while it asks from him an individual personal response, nevertheless the end which it is seeking cannot really be even partially comprehended in terms of the individual alone. As surely as men are all the children of the one divine Father, and can fulfill the true end of their life only by being in fellowship with him, so also they are members one of another and can fulfill the true end of their life only by being in fellowship with one another. This is but to restate in another way what was spoken of in an earlier chapter, namely, that the personal world always has two poles, so that an individual is always related to God and his neighbor at the same time, and a new relationship to the one must also be a new relationship to the other. But the point I want now to emphasize is that the Christian doctrine of the love of God necessarily carries with it the thought that that love is set toward the building up of a *community* just as much as toward the salvation of the individual. Indeed these are not two ends, but one—a new individual means, in principle, a new community, and effective saving action on the part of God into the midst of history must there-

---

in the former. In its insistence that the forgiveness of sinful persons constitutes a problem worthy of God, in its insistence on its cost, its difficulty, its cosmic significance, it once again puts the world of persons right at the center of the picture.

fore mean the bringing into existence of a new community the midst of history.

This is important, for it indicates the true basis of the Christian doctrine of the Church—a point on which so many, both inside and outside the Church, seem a little hazy. *The idea of the Church is part of the Christian doctrine of God.* The Church is not an optional adden- dum to the Christian way of life, and, as such, something which can be dispensed with. It is not something brought into existence by the social instinct of humanity, a sort of Christian get-together club. The divine purpose of love, in so far as it achieves its end of bringing human persons back to the real meaning of their life, calls into being, and must call into being, a new order of personal relationship. It creates a new fellowship of men and women which is both the realization and the organ of its purpose in history—so far as that purpose, which in the end must transcend history, is realizable on the plane of history at all. The distinctive mark of this new community is precisely that it is called to embody *agape*—that is to say, a love which, making no distinctions whatever, loves men because they are there, and because God so loves them. Thus the apostle Paul writes that in the Church there is neither "Greek nor Jew, circum- cision nor uncircumcision, Barbarian, Scythian, bond nor free."

No doubt the Church has constantly fallen, and constantly does fall, deplorably far short of this ideal; but at least she recognizes herself to be under its judgment and rebuke, which is a great deal. The point I want to emphasize, however, is that the notion—still sometimes encountered—that it is possible to be a Christian and have little or no connection with the Christian Church is flatly contrary to the mind of Christ and of the New Testament. The doctrine of the Church, I repeat, is part of the distinctive Christian doctrine of God revealed as love in Jesus Christ—God the Father of our Lord Jesus Christ. It is part also of its distinctive teaching concerning the divine-human personal world.

## V

In view of all that has been said hitherto, we can hardly avoid some reference to the question whether we are entitled to believe that, in the final consummation of God's purpose, *all* persons will be saved.

It helps to prevent misunderstanding and unnecessary discussion if we make clear to ourselves how the question arises. It does not arise out of a merely speculative interest in matters which lie beyond our knowledge and responsibility; nor does it arise out of a merely sentimental aversion to those austerities of the divine judgment upon, and dealing with, sin which are plainly enough manifest in this world—altogether apart from what may happen beyond it—and which may be comprehended, as we have seen, under the notion of the divine wrath. It arises out of the whole Christian message concerning God and man, and out of the necessities of that new life of trust in God and love to men to which the Christian is called by God's message to him.

For Christian faith requires that God's purpose should

be victorious; it urgently needs to affirm, and to rest on, the sovereignty and omnicompetence of God. It requires also that there should be no departure from the doctrine that God is *agape,* that his is a love which goes out to all persons merely because they are there as persons, a love which in its historic self-manifestation in Jesus Christ shows itself as seeking and saving the lost at any cost to itself. Yet how could the divine love be accounted omnicompetent and victorious, how could it be thought to suffer any other than the most grievous defeat if vast numbers of persons are finally lost in some sort of hell or —as some have suggested—by total annihilation? The same problem presents itself if we try to picture the state of the redeemed in the realized kingdom of God which we call heaven. The redeemed man is the man who has been brought to share the divine love for persons. How then can there be heaven for such a one if even one person is finally lost? The existence of hell surely makes heaven impossible. These are not dialectical points; they are, so to say, part of the logic of love in the Christian sense of that term. Anybody who does not feel the pressure of these questions must have completely failed to understand, or to accept, what I have been trying to set forth in the previous pages.

Why not, then, embrace without further ado a doctrine of the final restoration of all persons? Three things properly make us hesitate. I will state them and make one or two comments on each.

First, it is absolutely necessary, as we have more than once insisted, to preserve man's status as a person; in particular we must preserve his freedom, for without freedom he cannot be a person at all. Does not this necessarily involve the possibility that some men in their freedom may resist God to all eternity, or may reject him in some final way on which there is no going back? On this I make two comments.

(1) For one thing, we must not allow ourselves to think of freedom in a way that in effect isolates a man from his world, especially that close-knit world of relationships with other persons, both human and divine, which his existence as a person requires just as much as it requires freedom. As I have put it elsewhere,[4] to have the freedom of being a person is certainly not to exist in a vacuum of unrelatedness. It is manifest from our everyday experience that countless influences, pressures, appeals, compulsions of circumstances, and other things quite impossible to trace enter into all our choices and decisions; yet not so that the decision ceases to be in some real sense *our* decision, or to contain, so to say, something of our own causality. Sometimes, on looking back, we know that—though the decision was ours, and we must accept responsibility for it—we had in fact come to a point where we were, as the saying is, shut up to it; life had so unfolded, circumstances had so conspired, influences had so molded us, painful disciplines had so taught us, that we could not but see the truth at that point and walk in the way it directed; and thus an entirely new chapter in our personal history was opened up for us.

May not God, then, in his manifold wisdom bring

[4] *Towards Belief in God* (1942), p. 221.

even the most evil and recalcitrant soul to a situation, either in this world or the next, where the truth is presented with such compelling force and with such coincidental co-operation of internal conditions, that it cannot be resisted any longer—a situation where he can do no other than surrender at last?

Some such process, of necessity entailing much suffering—such as God in the austerity of his love does not scruple to allow and to use—we can indeed in some measure observe going on under our own own eyes in this present life. Anyone who has worked with sick and neurotic minds knows how often it is of the sheer mercy of God that, after running away from truth and reality for years, at last they find everything crashing about their ears; and, furthermore, what an important part in the process of profiting by the crash must be played by the personal help which they may get from one who skillfully understands, with love and candor, their history and interior life. And every Christian can look back on his life and marvel again and again at what little he can observe of God's wise and austere disciplining of him to new insights and responses all down the years—here a frustration or disappointment or failure, which at the time he would have done anything to avoid, there a chance meeting, somewhere else a coincidence of inner need and outward provision. And how much also there must be which is not observed at all. Yet never for one moment does he apprehend that there has been any infringement of his personal freedom. These things are the veriest commonplaces of the Christian life. They show that our freedom, without ceasing to be freedom, is so conditioned by inward and outward factors that God can and does save and sanctify us—often through great suffering.

(2) This leads to the second comment. We are bound to believe that God does in fact find a way of saving some persons that does not infringe their status as persons. We are bound to believe, too, that their salvation is wholly of God, so that if free response is a factor in it —as it must be—then it is a free response which is nevertheless made possible and evoked by God's dealings with them. If, then, God is able to do this with some, there would appear to be no reason to think that he cannot or will not do it with all, unless indeed we are prepared to accept the Calvinist view that God arbitrarily selects some for salvation and rejects others. Such a view of God's dealings with persons so depersonalizes the whole relationship, and is so totally contrary to what I have tried to set forth in these pages as the distinctive essence of the Christian message, that I must be permitted to reject it without discussion.

2. The second consideration which makes many hesitant to accept a doctrine of the final restoration of all persons is that they judge that such a doctrine takes away the urgency of the Christian message. Does not the doctrine give men carte blanche to indulge themselves as much as they like and as long as they like, seeing that, whatever they do, it will all come to the same thing in the end, namely salvation for all? And does it not, for the same reason, remove the urgent necessity to preach the gospel? These objections appear, at first hearing, to carry

172

considerable weight; nevertheless they spring, I believe, from a failure to grasp the distinctive Christian view of the nature of the personal world and God's purpose in it.

Let it be remembered that the Christian message does not merely announce God's saving work for men; it announces rather his saving work at *infinite cost*. At the heart of its message is the Incarnation and the Cross. Clearly, the man who could see in the ultimate triumph of the divine love at such cost an excuse for unlimited indulgence would merely reveal by so doing the utter darkness in which he dwells and his desperate need for a profound change of mind. And no shaking of him over the pit would bring him to that change of mind, for it would be but another appeal to the very selfishness which is already blinding his eyes. The most that the threat of possible damnation can do is to arrest the sinner in his evil ways; but in fact men are much more effectively arrested by immediate sufferings than by the thought of remote ones, however dreadful. To such more immediate sufferings in God's dealings with men we have certainly not denied a place; nevertheless even they cannot provide that positive illumination of the darkness of the soul which is the prime need. Some other way has to be found to bring home to a man the *intrinsic* urgency of the claim of God and his neighbor upon him. To this an appeal to the urgency of saving one's own skin will contribute nothing; it may indeed be a hindrance.

In a similar way the Christian believer who argues that without belief in a possible ultimate damnation there is no urgency to preach the gospel also reveals a failure to grasp the real nature of the personal order, and the claim of God and neighbor which meets us through it. The claim of my neighbor to my love, and God's claim on me through his claim, meet me as soon as I encounter him and merely because he is there as a person; it is contingent, so to say, only upon his presence, and not in any way upon what may or may not be his ultimate destiny. Furthermore, the fact that God will ultimately save all, if it is a fact, does not absolve me from responsibility in the matter; to suppose that it does is to have much too individualistic a view of the nature of personality. If all we have said hitherto about the bipolar structure of the personal world is true, then God's purpose of saving my neighbor cannot possibly be achieved merely by bringing him into a new relationship with himself; it can be achieved only by bringing my neighbor and me together into a new relationship with himself as well as with one another. In the restoration of that bipolar personal order to what God intends it to be I must therefore as a redeemed man play an indispensable part and to it I must bring an essential contribution; that part and contribution, so far as this present world is concerned, is the preaching of the gospel in word and life and deed.

The third consideration which makes many hesitant to accept a universalist view of God's saving purpose with men is that there are certain passages in the New Testament, notably in the recorded utterances of Jesus

Christ [5] which seem to suggest or imply the contrary. It is not possible to discuss these passages in detail here; they certainly ought not to be taken uncritically and at their face value, for the right interpretation of them raises many difficult exegetical problems—such as, for example, the influence of contemporary apocalyptic imagery, the meaning of the Greek word translated "everlasting" in the English version, the use of hyperbole in Hebrew idiom in order to obtain emphasis, and so on. I will content myself with saying three things. First, even if we grant, as perhaps we must, that the New Testament passages referred to imply at least the possibility of a person's being finally lost, that still leaves it open whether in fact any person actually will be so lost. We may suppose—if this is not to picture the matter too anthropomorphically—that in creating an order of free persons God took the risk of hell, but that it is within the compass of his manifold wisdom and sacrificial love to circumvent the risk and to save all, as we must believe he has in fact saved some. Second, there are other passages in the New Testament, notably in Paul's epistles, which seem definitely to suggest and imply a universal restoration of all men.[6] Third, though the New Testament thus gives no clear lead on the matter, nevertheless it very plainly lays great emphasis on the tremendous importance of what men do here and now in history— particularly in relation to Christ—and on the repercus-

[5] For example, Mark 9:43-48, Matt. 25:46.
[6] For references and discussion see C. H. Dodd, *The Epistle to the Romans*, "The Moffatt New Testament Commentary," pp. 183-84.

sions of that in what lies beyond history. If the New Testament is joyously certain of the boundless grace and resources of God, it is equally certain of a man's power continually to resist God in the working out of his purpose, with serious consequences to himself and to his fellows; though as to the limits of that resistance it gives, I repeat, no clear guidance.

To sum up: There seems no conclusive reason why we should not follow the logic of our belief in the love and sovereignty of God and affirm the restoration of all into unity with God and with one another; but if we do affirm it, we must not regard the bare idea of restoration as an adequate description of the final consummation. We are bound to add that it will be a restoration which contains within it both an infinite cost to God and also the unimpaired significance of human choices and decisions in time. Or, to state the matter the other way round, we must affirm the crucial importance of the soul's confrontation with Christ, so that it is true to say that if anyone ever did finally reject Christ, that would mean to be finally cut off from God. Yet we are never able to know whether anyone ever has, or ever will, finally reject Christ; and that being so, we are ready—knowing what God has achieved in our own lives in spite of what we have been and are—to commit everyone in trust and confidence to him. To adapt some words of Althaus: We must think of every man with both types of thought at the same time. By so doing we show that we are not in the realm of merely abstract, theoretical considerations at all, but in the realm of the living breath of our Christian life—its rest and its unrest, its peace and yet its struggle, its fearful sense of the tension of decision yet its confidence in the complete victory of God. This is the polarity of all thought about the final consummation—we take our stand in the eternal, in that which lies beyond the struggle, beyond the still undetermined possibilities of history, as though they were already determined; and yet at the same time we are immersed in history with all the cares and the worries and the responsibilities of choice for or against the rule of God.[7]

[7] *Die letzten Dinge* (1933) , p. 188.

# CHAPTER VII

# SKEPTICISM AND FAITH

WE have said that Christian teaching insists firmly on what we have called the holiness or "God-ness" of God. He is the omnipresent, omniscient, omnicompetent, sovereign, creative Will, utterly transcending our understanding, in whose grasp the whole creation lies, "of whom and through whom and to whom are all things." We have said, further, that the Christian revelation brings its special and all-transforming contribution to this doctrine of God by characterizing him also as the Father of our Lord Jesus Christ; the God who is creatively at work in the world and in all human history is, in respect of his relation to persons, fatherly love—interpreting both these words in the light of Jesus Christ.

It is characteristic of the Christian view that it holds these two things together. On the one hand—to take them in the reverse order—by its doctrine of the fatherly love of God it puts the individual person right in the center of the picture and steadfastly holds him there; God as fatherly love values every human person and is at work in his life, seeking to bring him, in ways consonant with his status as personal, into that fellowship and cooperation with the divine will which are his only true freedom and blessedness. On the other hand, God has made the whole vast order of nature, and has set moving the ongoing complex process of collective human history. He is at work in these also; they mean something to him, and he purposes something through them.

To my mind there is something quite daring in the way in which Christian faith has held steadfastly to both these things—to the assertion, that is, that the one transcendent divine purpose holds in its grasp the whole created universe and all the long ages of history and at the same time is unweariedly interested in individual men and women. It is indeed a grasping of the nettle with both hands. For when you contemplate nature and history, it is not at all easy to believe that there is a sovereign power at work in them which is interested in individuals as such—least of all in a way that might be even remotely characterized as loving. Is not the prime source of all the unsatisfied yearnings and heartaches—and sometimes despair—of sensitive human souls all down the ages to be found just here, namely, in this apparent frightful contradiction between the outward order of nature and history and the individual's inward sense of his own status and dignity as a person? It is this, surely, which is the source of what has been called the tragic sense of life, never more heavy upon us, perhaps, than now.

That the Christian faith should thus grasp the nettle and hold it might be urged as at least a hint—if nothing more—that there is at the heart of that faith a uniquely compelling and self-authenticating source of light and truth, which it would be foolishness in any man to pass by or to dismiss too easily. For, be it noted, the conviction that there is behind all things a wholly trustworthy love has emphatically not been confined, as is sometimes suggested, either to the comfortably-off bourgeois classes or, on the other hand, to dull and half-defeated souls who, in their poverty and misery, have wanted an opiate for their sorrows. It has just as often gripped and transformed the lives of vigorous and sincere men and women who have both faced in thought and grappled with in action the challenging facts in all their anguish and mystery. The apostle Paul is a case in point—to mention only one example.

I propose that in this concluding chapter we try to face frankly this challenge which at once presents itself to our minds when we put the individual life in the setting of the whole vast process of nature and history and seek to envisage both as grasped and ruled by one and the same sovereign love. I propose that we do this for two reasons: first, it is important that in the presentation of our message we do not lay ourselves open to the charge that we have ignored, or are unwilling to face, the difficulties of belief; second, and more important, to do so may help to clarify, and perhaps deepen, our understanding of what the Christian faith essentially is, and of what sustains it.

Let us set forth the contrast—if that is not too mild a word—between, on the one hand, the impression that nature and history make upon us as we look out upon them and, on the other hand, the Christian assertion that there is at work in both a sovereign love interested in individual men and women; and let us, in our brief statement of this contrast, be as vivid and uncompromising as we can—even at the risk of overstatement. We will first put the case for unbelief—and allow full rein to that skeptical voice which I confess sometimes whispers in the back of my mind whenever I hear anyone say, or whenever I myself say, "God is love."

God is love? Consider, then, the voice might comment, the vast, vast amplitude of the sheerly material universe, particularly as modern research has disclosed it to us. Consider the infinite universes of the heavens, the innumerable, literally unimaginable multitudes of the planets and stars, their unthinkable distances, measurable only in light-years, their incredible age, the unfathomable abysses of empty space, and amid it all our own infinitesimal earth, smaller in comparison, infinitely smaller, than a grain of dust. What of the vast whirling nebulae, the flying comets that appear out of the void and vanish again, the flaming stars, the stars that are cooling, and still more the stars which hang out there in space frozen and dead. Think only of the sun, one among ten million such, and ten million times ten million, a vast globe of superheated gas, blazing, roaring, hurtling through limitless space for ten million and ten million times ten million years. Or— stranger still in some ways—consider that flat, cold disc of the moon staring down upon us, suspended there in the night sky, so silent, so lifeless. What does it all mean, what can it all mean? How does the love of the personal God fit into it all?

Or come nearer home, the voice might continue. Consider the dark inscrutabilities of nature as it immediately environs our lives. Consider deluge, earthquake, tornado, volcano, and all the violent and eruptive destructiveness of our world; not only do these crash in upon our human lives and human undertakings, making mockery of them, but they are utterly baffling in themselves. Why should there be a long process of evolutionary creation involving all this conflict and interplay of titanic forces— cooling crusts, ice ages, arctic wastes, the surging oceans, the blistering deserts, hideous monsters battling in the primeval swamps? Or consider the prolific, wasteful, and fiercely competitive fecundity of life on this planet alone— the mind reels at the thought. What a blank incomprehensibility is the enormous busyness of an ant heap or a wasp hole! What mystery looks out through the gentle eyes of a dog, or through the cold beady eyes of a cobra, or sounds through the howling of wolves on the chase! Why the wart hog, the tarantula, the cholera microbe, the hookworm?

How does the love of the personal God fit into all these?

> Tiger, tiger, burning bright
> In the forests of the night,
> What immortal hand or eye,
> Could frame thy fearful symmetry?
>
> .  .  .  .  .  .  .  .  .
>
> Did He smile His work to see?
> Did He who made the lamb make thee?

Or finally, the voice might conclude, consider the long ages of human history as modern knowledge has brought these vividly before us. The endless, endless procession of the generations of mankind, being born, suffering bitterly so many of them, living at most a few short years, and then dying, century after century—from the primitive savage beating his tom-tom, quailing before his witch doctor, and burying men alive in the grave of the chief, through the great civilizations which have risen and passed into nothingness and are now only a few moldering stones in a field where rabbits breed and feed, to this present civilization, latest product of what some are pleased to think of as progress, with its atomic bombs dropped on teeming cities, its slaughter of thousands of young lives, its massacre of Jews, and all the horrors of this time. What does it all mean, where is it all leading—the anguish, the cruelty, the disorder, the tumult, the chaos, the frustration, the swift transiency of human affairs—the seemingly endless and meaningless going on, and turning back, and perpetual getting nowhere of it all? Fit the personal love of God, if you can, into that picture!

What is the reply to all this? It is certainly not any attempt to provide a theory which shall so explain and illumine the mystery and darkness that none is left; Christianity has never attempted to do that, though Christian thinkers have succeeded in saying, in the light of the Christian revelation, some things which shed a glimmer of light here and there. No, the reply is to ask for a deeper understanding of what the Christian faith essentially is and whence it is derived.

# I

First, it is important to insist, with ourselves and with those to whom we speak, that the Christian gospel has from the beginning claimed to rest on God's own active

GOD AND MEN

*disclosure* of himself in the midst of our world as holy love. The Christian gospel is not, strictly speaking, the simple statement that God is love; it is rather that God himself discloses, exhibits, commends, makes credible, his nature and purpose as love to us through Christ, and very especially through Christ's death on the cross. The Christian faith has certainly never claimed that the proposition that God is sovereign love is self-evident to the human mind. That would be absurd, for quite plainly it is *not* self-evident; judging, indeed, by the history of religions, the only statement about God which comes near to being self-evident to the human mind is that he is inscrutable power. Nor has it claimed that God's love can be inferred or proved from, or read out of, the facts of nature or history; indeed, it fully admits that from the point of view of many of these facts the doctrine has very little credibility, if any at all.

*That is precisely why it needs to be revealed.* It is God, and God alone, who has disclosed his character and purpose toward us—in Jesus Christ. It is God, and God alone, who has broken through the thick clouds which veil his being and has permitted us to see his heart. It is God, and God alone, who has sent forth this light out of the midst of the otherwise impenetrable darkness and mystery by which we are surrounded. Whoso says Christianity says revelation. If the doctrine of the love of God is not revelation which God himself increasingly authenticates to any who, feeling in the least degree its compelling power, will commit themselves to it in faith, Christianity has very little it can say in answer to the voice we were listening to

184

a minute ago. From this point of view the Christian gospel seems to me to be realistically consistent with our actual situation. It does not say that history teaches us, or nature teaches us, or science teaches us, or the events of our own times teach us, or that our hearts teach us, that God is love; for it knows very well they do nothing of the sort. It says, that God has of himself, and by his own intiative and act, told us this about himself, namely, that he is holy love.

We may put it another way by saying that the Christian faith claims that in Jesus Christ the light has shined out of darkness. It *is* darkness out of which it shines, and in many ways it remains darkness; nevertheless it *is* light that is given, and to those who choose to walk in it, it is light enough. Or we may put it in still another way by saying that Christianity, while it claims to give knowledge, asks always for a certain humble agnosticism in a man's thought about God, and in his attitude toward God. As was said in the preceding chapter, it never allows us to forget that when we talk of the love of God, we are speaking not only of love but also of God—the infinite and eternal creator, unfathomable in the awful mystery of his being. He is not the less this for being love; but also he is not the less love for being this. He is God and not man.

In this connection we may point out a certain foolish anthropomorphism which may be detected lurking behind our skeptical voices comments. These comments continually hint that there is an intrinsic absurdity in the idea that so vast a universe should have at its heart an all-comprehending and individualizing wisdom and love

—a wisdom and love which knows and has a concern for every man, woman, and child born on this infinitesimal speck called earth. Yet obviously the argument might well run, and indeed ought to run, in precisely the opposite direction. Just because the universe is on so vast a scale, it is surely in a way easier to maintain that the power which has fashioned it, and holds it together as a universe, so that it does not collapse into final chaos, might know and love every finite person it has called into existence—numbering, as the Bible says, "the very hairs of his head." To suppose otherwise is surely to think of God after the image of the managing director of a department store, who has far too many important affairs on his hands to know anything about the charwoman who scrubs the passages.

I remember reading, some years ago, an even cruder example of what is essentially the same argument in a newspaper article. The writer, a distinguished scientist, solemnly said that he just could not believe in the survival after death of all human persons because such an unthinkably large number of them must have lived since the beginning of history. I do not know quite what was intended by such a naïve piece of thinking. I can only suppose that the implication was that there would not be room for them all. Yet one would have imagined—if one is to think of these matters in spatial terms at all, which perhaps one should not do—that a universe whose distances we can only dimly comprehend in terms of light-years might be able to get us all in without undue overcrowding.

Nevertheless, even though there is no need to aggravate our difficulties by childish arithmetical anthropomorphisms of the kind just described, there remain both the impossibility of *inferring* the love of God from the facts of nature and of history and the need for a divine revelation. In accordance with this the Christian message has always insisted that the proper response to the revelation given in Christ is something which it calls "faith." Faith is that attitude of mind which, finding itself laid hold of by the truth concerning God's love as given through Christ, commits itself to that truth in adventurous trust and obedience, in spite of all the mystery and all the perplexity that remain. Discerning the love of God at work at that one point in historical time, the Christian is prepared to trust it over all history, all time; discerning it at that one point in space, he is prepared to trust it—as it were—in all places whatsoever, and over all space; discerning it at work in that particular complex of personal relationships which constitutes the earthly life of Jesus, he is prepared to trust it to be at work in all personal relationships whatsoever. Moreover, only in such adventurous trust and experimental obedience—particularly in the sphere of personal relationships—can the truth that God is love be authenticated to the soul and built up into a massive conviction, despite all the mystery and darkness. So the apostle Paul, after meditating on what he calls "the groaning and travailing together of the whole creation," is yet able to write what is surely the grandest expression of faith in all literature—an expression which is the more grand for burking none of the facts:

187

Who shall separate us from the love of Christ? shall tribulation, or distress, or persecution, or famine, or nakedness, or peril, or sword? . . . I am persuaded that neither death, nor life, nor angels, nor principalities, nor powers, nor things present, not things to come [shall we say, no dimension of time, no long-drawn-out enigma of history?] nor height nor depth [shall we say, no dimension of space, no infinite immeasurability of the suns and the stars?] nor any other creature, shall be able to separate us from the love of God which is in [which meets us in, discloses itself to us through] Jesus Christ our Lord.

## II

Second, in our presentation of the gospel it is important to give due weight to the fact that the Christian message of the love of God manifested in Jesus Christ does not run away from, or minimize, or gloss over, the cruel and challenging facts of our world and of human history. The revealing action of God, according to that message, culminates in Calvary; that is to say, in an event so cruel and so challenging that the voice of skepticism could scarcely cite anything worse. It culminates in the brutal flogging and agonizing execution of a young man—a young man who, be it noted, had lived his life in the faith that God is wholly trustworthy love; the whole vile thing being brought about by the alliance of political and ecclesiastical trickery with brutal military power and a propagandized mob inflamed with national feeling.

Once again we must insist that the Christian message is not simply that God is love; it is that God has revealed his love in Jesus Christ, and Jesus Christ is Jesus Christ horribly crucified—there is no other. That is to say, according to the Christian faith, when God discloses himself as love, he does not in the least lead us away from the terrible things which happen in history. He does not say, "Come away from the horror of things and take a look at the daffodils and crocuses in the springtime; let them speak to you of my goodness." On the contrary he leads us right into the very midst of the horror of things, and *meets us there;* he speaks to us out of the heart of the darkness. No, let us never forget that at the center of the Christian gospel is the Cross. The gospel is not lyrical sentimentality about the loveliness of the world; it is not saccharin stuff about being "nearer to God's heart in a garden than anywhere else on earth"; that is a very typical bourgeois sentiment, and it simply is not true, unless, indeed, we are thinking—as the writer of it certainly was not—of the Garden of Gethsemane, where one was in such dire agony of soul that it is written of him that the sweat fell from him as it had been blood.

There is indeed a profound and realistic adequacy here in the Christian message, which can hardly be denied, even though the message may not be believed. After all, suppose it is true that God is holy love; it may well be true —there is nothing intrinsically absurd or impossible in the idea itself. Suppose, too, that God, being love, did purpose to get it across to men in such a way that they could become, and could remain, possessed of the truth of it, no matter what evil of darkness could overtake them. How would he do it—how could he do it? Short of hypnotizing men into believing it, which would not be treating them as persons, or short of shattering the world to bits and making another of an entirely different kind, which God no doubt has good reasons for not doing, it would seem that there is only one way in which he could achieve such a purpose. That one way would be for him to thrust home the truth about himself to our hearts in and through and out of the heart of just those things which seem most fiercely to question it. This, according to the Christian faith, is part at least of what God did at Calvary. If God causes the light to shine out of that sort of darkness, what other conceivable darkness can ever suffice to blot it out?

Many years ago as a young man I was preaching on the love of God; there was in the congregation an old Polish Jew who had been converted to the Christian faith. He came to me afterward and said, "You have no right to speak of the love of God until you have seen, as I have seen, a massacre of Jews in Poland—until you have seen, as I have seen, the blood of your dearest friends running in the gutters on a gray winter morning." I asked him later how it was that, having seen such a massacre, *he* had come to believe in the love of God. The answer he gave in effect was that the Christian gospel first began to lay hold of him because it bade him see God—the love of God—as it were, just where he was, just where he could not but always be in his thought and memories—in those blood-stained streets on that gray morning. It bade him see the love of God, not somewhere else, but in the midst of just that sort of thing, in the blood and agony of Calvary. He did at least know, he said, that this was a message that grappled with the facts; and then he went on to say something the sense of which I shall always remember though the words I have forgotten. He said, "As I looked at that man upon the cross, as I heard him pray, 'Father, forgive them; for they know not what they do,' as I heard him cry in his anguish, 'My God, my God, why hast thou forsaken me?' and yet thereafter say, 'Father, into thy hands I commend my spirit,' I knew I was at a point of final crisis and decision in my life; I knew I must make up my mind once and for all, and either take my stand beside him and share in his undefeated faith in God—committing myself to the transcendent clarity of the vision of one so infinitely purer than myself—or else fall finally into a bottomless pit of bitterness, hatred, and unutterable despair."

### III

Third, as we face the darkness and mystery of the world and of human history, it is important to remind ourselves and our hearers of what we have more than once spoken of already, namely, that God's action in the world, and in particular his coming into history in Jesus Christ, is not yet, according to the Christian faith, a completed and fully consummated action. On the contrary, Christianity has always said that whatever it is that the infinite God is doing in and through this mysterious universe—its whirling suns and stars, the teeming life of nature, the tumult and chaos of history, our individual lives so swiftly running out into the silence of death—whatever it is he is doing in his wisdom and love and power, it will only finally be achieved in a kingdom which lies beyond and transcends this observable world of space and time. There is an unfathomable "beyond" to it all; the purpose of the eternal God must be something infinitely bigger than this present finite, tiny world. No doubt, when God's kingdom comes, it will take up into itself, and justify, all the long travail involved in the creation and history of this planet; but it will not itself be contained in that creation and history.

We spoke of this earlier when we were considering modern views of progress, with their naïve faith in a perfect end state of human life to be realized at some future date on this earth. We saw how this inevitably degrades the personal status of those who live meanwhile but who, in the nature of the case, will never participate in the end state of perfection when it comes. As against this we said that it is part of the radical personalism of Christianity that it puts the realized kingdom of God beyond history—for only thus can the personal value which the love of God bestows on the individual man or woman be preserved.

We now come back to the same truth from a different angle; it all fits together. The point now is that if the divine purpose of love transcends history, as it must, then for us who are still in history there must remain a considerable darkness and mystery which will entirely baffle our understanding; to expect anything else would be like expecting to understand the deep meaning of a Shakespearean tragedy by reading only the first scene. The Christian believer, therefore, by the very terms of his faith, is not baffled and defeated by the darkness and confusion, the apparent meaninglessness, of the world he looks out upon; indeed, in a measure he expects it, and so is reconciled to it, for he knows that the world's real and final meaning lies beyond itself. But he is sure of one thing, and that is that within and above all is God's sovereign and undefeatable love. The Christian is thus called to live in the peace and power of "the world to come."

But, be it noted, this conviction that the final realization of the divine kingdom lies beyond this world—so that what God is doing in this world cannot be understood in terms of what is observable in this world, but must always wear in some measure an inscrutable face to us—does not make this present world a merely dark and meaningless affair, which we must get through as quickly as we can and the more quickly the better. Such a false and selfish unworldliness has nothing whatever to do with Christianity, though it has often masqueraded under its name. For, clearly, it is utterly contrary to the Christian insistence that God's claim for our trust and obedience meets us here and now in the claim of the neighbor to our love. God's claim upon us in the here and the now of history is not any the less claim because in and through that claim he is fashioning us for, and calling us into, a kingdom whose final consummation lies beyond history. On the contrary, this otherworldly aspect brings an added solemnity to the claim. It is in this world, here and now, and in the living of a right human life in it, that the redeemed man—redeemed that is, through the revelation in Christ—is under the rule of God and has fellowship with him; he already lives in that kingdom of love and light which in its realized fullness is yet to be. This brings us to the fourth and final point.

## IV

If a man is in any degree now to enter into that kingdom of God, to come under that rule of God, which in its fullness is yet to be, then it is most necessary that he should continually submit himself to the revelation given in Christ of the way in which God works in the world. He must be prepared radically to rethink his notions of what the true values of life are, and wherein they are to be found. That will not be easy, but there is no escaping it, for part of the Christian answer to the confusion and suffering and perplexity of life—and perhaps the most important part of it—is that men need desperately to have their sin-blinded vision cleared. Many things are dark and mysterious in themselves, for the reasons we have given, and we must be content to wait for light upon them; but they are made more dark by the distortions of our own minds. The shadow that rests upon our lives is always in some measure cast by ourselves.

To take only one central example: There is one craving and expectancy which all men bring with them to the interpretation of life, and which they must get rid of if God's rule in the world is to be understood at all; it is extremely hard to get rid of it, and for most of us it needs a continuous effort of mind. It is the craving and expectancy that God should rule men's lives on a basis of strict distributive justice. The natural man has an incurably legalistic and prize-distribution mind; God, he says, ought to bring it about that appropriate rewards are given to the good people and appropriate penalties to the evil ones —such rewards and penalties being pictured for the most part in terms of the good and bad things of life in this world. The man who lives a good life ought to receive, in proportional degree, present prosperities and delights; the man who does not live a good life ought to receive, in proportional degree, the reverse. How deep-seated this craving is needs no pointing out to anybody who has any power to observe his own mental processes. The first and most repeated criticism of life which falls from the lips of a child is usually, "It isn't fair," and the habit persists with most people to the end. "What have I done to deserve this trouble?" they cry. "What has he done to deserve that success? Why do the innocent suffer for the guilty? Why do the guilty prosper by the sufferings of the innocent? It isn't fair." People *ought* to get their deserts. If they do not—and quite obviously they do not; the facts are plain and undeniable—then the question is, "What is God doing? How can we have any assurance that God is ruling the world?"

There are a number of things which might be said about this, and which there is not space to say here; some of them have been hinted at in previous chapters. But the deepest and most challenging thing that the Christian faith has to say is that if a man would really fulfill God's purpose for him, and pass through this world in deepening fellowship with, and assurance of, God—thus having something of the stature of a mature son of God—then he must come right out of this legalistic world of rewards and penalties conceived in terms of the good things of this life, and never allow himself for one moment to slip back into it. Only if he does this, can he be freed once and for all from that resentment, frustration, and darkness of soul which has its final outcome in unbelief. For, quite certainly, God does not arrange life on the basis of nicely adjusted rewards and penalties; moreover no one who has even so much as begun to discern the truth about God and men which has been given us through Christ would ever want him to do so.

The Christian man discerns that the real blessedness of human life is in that personal fellowship with God which comes as a man shares in God's purpose of saving love in the world, and not in anything else. It is not a matter of first doing God's will and sharing his purpose and then getting a reward of another sort added on; rather it is that in the doing of his will and the sharing of his purpose the true end of man's life as a person is achieved, and nothing else in comparison with that really matters. "My meat," said Christ, "is to do the will of God"; the meat is not added afterward as a reward. When once this high and difficult truth is glimpsed, however falteringly, then it becomes possible to know—and to have peace in the knowledge—that the worst deprivation or disaster need be no contradiction of the good purpose of God. The deep shadows of life cease to be rewards unjustly withheld or penalties unjustly inflicted; they become rather a challenge to a new understanding of, or, where understanding is still lacking, to a new trust in, his ways. But this emancipating insight is not possible so long as we remain obstinately in a world of distributive justice.

There is no more impressive expression of this profound truth than that which is to be found in the words which Jesus put into the mouth of the father at the end of the parable of the prodigal son. The words are the more impressive for being so simple and natural and unforced—thus showing how utterly different was the world in which our Lord habitually lived and moved from that in which most of us are content to dwell.

The elder brother, on the other hand, perfectly incarnates that mind which, in its thought of God, is working wholly with a legalistic scheme of distributive justice. Witness his words when he hears that the wastrel young brother has not been given his deserts: "Lo, these many years do I serve thee, neither transgressed I at any time thy commandments"—pure legalism, the exact performance of commandments. "Thou never gavest me a kid"—rewards in terms of the good things of this life, a claim for them established and handed in. "That I might make merry with my friends"—the sphere of reward is not in the personal relationship with the father, but somewhere else; "This thy son was come"—little love in that; the word "thy" stands the fellow over there, apart from me, merely another competitor in the prize distribution. Now observe the answer, and how it throws into the sharpest possible relief the whole distinctive nature of this new understanding of God's ways: A kid, indeed! "Son, *all* that I have is thine"—the divine love is reaching out in self-giving all the time, in respect of everything. With

your friends! "Thou art ever *with me*"—the highest and
final blessedness of man is to be with God, nothing else in
comparison really matters. "This thy son is come"! "This
thy *brother* was dead, and is alive again; and was lost, and
is found"—if a man is to be "with God," then he must
share in God's saving purpose of love toward his fellows.
With what superlative art it is all condensed into so few
simple words; the very naturalness and simplicity of the
words are evidence of their truth.

As soon as a man steps right out of the realm of distributive justice, and sets on one side the idea that rewards and
penalties are a clue to the understanding of the divine
government of the world, not only is he given an entirely
new attitude to such sufferings and deprivations as may
be his own lot, but also it becomes possible for him at least
to begin to see all the dire sufferings of men—all the long
anguish and travail and frustration of history—in a new
light. There will remain, even so, much darkness and
mystery—much to wring the heart, much to call for faith
—but at least it now becomes possible to believe, nay to
know, that God is using it all, and will use it all, to build
up a kingdom of persons in relationship—a kingdom
whose governing principle is not, I repeat, "justice" and
the awarding of prizes or penalties, but a sacrificial self-
giving which knows and desires no other good thing than
to be at one with God, and with all persons, in love. As
leading up to that consummation in the divine kingdom
which lies *beyond* history, all that men have suffered so
unequally and so perplexingly *in* history will at last be
seen to have been fully worth while, calling for no nice

compensating adjustments on the part of God, and no regrets on the part of men.

All this deep and challenging truth is summed up—once again—in the Cross of our Lord Jesus Christ. The Crucifixion is the most gross and shocking example of injustice in history; for he who was crucified was the only really innocent person who ever walked the earth. Yet God used the Cross to reveal to men's sin-blinded eyes the true meaning of their life and destiny, and to redeem men into his kingdom. Why? Because the meaning of our life and the final secret of God's kingdom is not in justice at all—as men rate justice—but in a sacrificial and self-giving love. "With his stripes we are healed." With his stripes the world of persons is healed

# INDEX

# INDEX

Temple, W., 88
Tennant, F. E., 109n
Total depravity, 95
Trust, 52-54, 60-61
Truth, its compellingness, 21-22

Universalism, 168-77
Unworldliness, 193-94
Urgency of gospel, 172-73

Values, 64-65

Wishful thinking, 34-37, 148-49
Wodehouse, H., 64n
World to come, 108-10, 193
Worship, 139

Zacchaeus, 165